ABDUL QUAYYUM KHAN KUNDI

Lessons from Quran

First edition

This book was professionally typeset on Reedsy.
Find out more at reedsy.com

Dedication
Dedicated to all those who strive for justice in their societies.

Contents

Preface

Philosophers agree that religion presents a higher truth which is beyond the reach of philosophy and science. Reasons alluded to are that science is limited to explaining nature and combination of things. Science is handicapped since it cannot create anything in a vacuum. Philosophy on the other hand is multidimensional striving to extend established boundaries of knowledge. Philosophy presents abstract ideas that are expected to be eventually rationalized through science, reason and logic. In achieving these objectives philosophers had to sometimes pay a high price. Socrates was condemned to drink from a chalice of poison while Galileo Galilei was incarcerated until his death. History is replete with stories of philosophers who were condemned for presenting ideas that were far ahead of contemporary thought.

Religion struggles to convey an immovable and unchangeable absolute truth which is beyond rational reaches of mind. This creates uncertainties that could have devastating consequences for mankind. Religion presents a truth that may not be comprehensible by intellect of mankind but is manifest in the sprawling universe in front of us. This universe is available to be explored by an unquenchable human curiosity to inquire about it. Philosophy and science will eventually reach a stage where it will be in unison with absolute truth. All philosophies and scientific discoveries are meant to serve mankind as no other creature in the universe either seeks it or adopts it voluntarily. This could be evidence that Truth without expressing itself in action is a mere vanity and amusement of mind.

The Quran, for Muslims, is a divine revelation that provides clues to evolve a higher state of consciousness. The Quran presented the idea that all creatures came from water long before Darwin and other evolutionary scientists arrived at that conclusion.

(Verse 21.030) Do not the Unbelievers see that the heavens and the earth were joined together (as one unit of creation), before we clove them asunder? We made from water every living thing. Will they not then believe?

Without rejecting or questioning the existence of a divine creator Darwin presented a theory which was a scientific confirmation of the Quran's instruction of evolution of species revealed in various verses. Building on this theory of evolution scientists have reached the conclusion that there was a big bang event from which emanates all that is in this universe and on earth. They have so far not been able to arrive at a conclusion about what was there before the big bang or what was the composition of dense matter that exploded to initiate infinite numbers of creative processes. The Quran provides a clue to this in the following verses:

(Verse 2.117) To Him is due the primal origin of the heavens and the earth: When He decreeth a matter, He saith to it: "Be," and it is.

(Verse 36.081) "Is not He Who created the heavens and the earth able to create the like thereof?" - Yea, indeed! for He is the Creator Supreme, of skill and knowledge (infinite)! **(Verse 36.082)** Verily, when He intends a thing, His Command is, "be", and it is!

Scientists have developed theories to explain the formation of celestial bodies and creation of life on earth in the aftermath of the big bang. Evolution happens not only in existing species but there is creation of new ones without damaging the ecological balance. No plant, insect, animal or a bird is without a place or purpose in the total equation that defines an environmental balance. Ironically it is only discoveries of men that have polluted environment. Genetic science should not be outside of human endeavor but failure at it could have devastating effect. It is important that safeguards are carefully considered before widespread experimentation is allowed.

Theory of evolution so far fails to identify the exact moment in time when a mutation happens in a gene and intelligence is increased in a species. Evolutionary science falls short of explaining why humans are the only species with a far superior intellect.

This knowledge is so powerful that it could develop spacecraft that travels to mars while all other beings struggle to even develop a well-structured language. As science studies building blocks of humanity through genetics and DNA it will find the factual story of human evolution without lope holes or broken strands. Until then we can consider clues provided by the Quran in many chapters and verses to explain the mystical story of creation of Adam. Here is the story of Adam from Chapter 2 Al Baqarah:

(Verse 2.030) Behold, thy Lord said to the angels: "I will create a vicegerent on earth." They said: "Wilt Thou place therein one who will make mischief therein and shed blood?- whilst we do celebrate Thy praises and glorify Thy holy (name)?" He said: "I know what ye know not." **(Verse 2.031)** And He taught Adam the names of all things; then He placed them before the angels, and said: "Tell me the names of these if ye are right." **(Verse 2.032)** They said: "Glory to Thee, of knowledge We have none, save what Thou Hast taught us: In truth it is Thou Who art perfect in knowledge and wisdom." **(Verse 2.033)** He said: "O Adam! Tell them their names." When he had told them, Allah said: "Did I not tell you that I know the secrets of heaven and earth, and I know what ye reveal and what ye conceal?" **(Verse 2.034)** And behold, We said to the angels: "Bow down to Adam" and they bowed down. Not so Iblis: he refused and was haughty: He was of those who reject Faith.

There are many observations that can be made from this narrative of the story of Adam. First is that man was endowed with intellect but unlike angels he had the authority to have a free will to use it without any predefined limits. That is probably why angels expressed fear that progeny of Adam can engage in violence and transgression. It is this exercise of free will that is tested in our daily lives. But the story does not end here. It continues when Adam exercises this free will for the first time. Here is how the Quran narrates it:

(Verse 2.035) We said: "O Adam! dwell thou and thy wife in the Garden; and eat of the bountiful things therein as (where and when) ye will; but approach not this tree, or ye run into harm and transgression." (Verse 2.036) Then did Satan make them slip from the (garden), and get them out of the state (of felicity) in which they had been. We said: "Get ye down, all (ye people), with enmity between yourselves. On earth will be your dwelling-place and your means of livelihood - for a time." **(Verse 2.037)** Then learnt Adam from his Lord words of inspiration, and his Lord Turned towards him; for He is Oft-Returning, Most Merciful. **(Verse 2.038)** We said: "Get ye down all from here; and if, as is sure, there comes to you Guidance from me, whosoever follows My guidance, on them shall be no fear, nor shall they grieve.

So now Adam with his powerful intellect and free will is set on its first test. It was not that the type of tree was important but that he was told that approaching it could be harmful. Anyone using common sense will suggest that a person with intellect and reason will abstain from an action that could be harmful. But alas that is exactly what he does. One wonders why he would do that. The Quran shed some light on it when Iblis (Satan) refused to bow down to Adam and was permitted to try to corrupt Adam, if he can. Iblis considered Adam inferior because clay was mentioned as a key ingredient of his composition. In many verses the Quran suggests that the reach of Iblis is limited only to making sinister suggestions without any power to force a person to commit a sin. Iblis challenged the intellect of Adam to know what new knowledge was hidden in the forbidden tree. This sense that some knowledge was beyond his reach was too much for Adam to bear since it was this capability that made him superior after all. This sheds light on the human condition which is not purely driven by logic and reason alone but rather gets a significant influence from emotions and feelings. These verses suggest that emotions in humans are formed from the interaction of knowledge, free will, and vagueness of an unknown or uncertain future. There is not a scientist or philosopher that can claim that they are free of emotions or feelings.

Adam succumbs to his curiosity by eating from the forbidden tree and immediately learns of his shame. Why is that? God tells him not to transgress this limit but does not inform him of the exact consequences of abrogating that command. After eating the forbidden fruit Adam learned to his shame that there was no new knowledge in it that he already did not have. This puts his intellect in a dilemma that if there was nothing new then why the Creator made it out of bounds for him. It was then that dawned on Adam that in issuing this command to make that tree beyond his reach was manifestation of the difference between the Creator and Created. With this realization came consciousness of shame of breaking covenant with the Creator, the grief of wronging oneself without getting any benefit or wisdom and the fear of a punishment for transgressing the prescribed limit.

Now we enter next phase in this story when God had to judge Adam for disobeying his command. This is expressed in Verse 2.036 & Verse 2.038 when God instructs Adam to get down to earth as well as predicts that there will be enmity between men. What does this mean? Why would rational and intelligent men commit violent crimes? The answer lies in the difference between heaven and earth as well as the terms of engagement for the progeny of Adam. In heaven Adam did not have to work for a livelihood to sustain himself so there was no competition for resources nor was there an expiry date to his abode in it. On earth he has to earn his livelihood as well as live for an uncertain but limited period of time which means an immeasurable supply of sustenance would be needed. Combination of these two factors i.e. an unknown term on earth and competition for resources became main source of enmity between men as we can see it play out in wars on a larger scale and our lives at a micro level.

In last part of verse 2.038 God gives hope to men that during his period of struggle on earth help will come in the form of guidance. This guidance comes in two ways. First, it is the education that a child gets to gain control of his faculties that are encoded in human DNA. A child in his genes carries intellect with which all mankind is endowed but it is hidden in deep recesses of the soul. To get it out requires the longest maturity period among all animals. A person attains adulthood in about 18 years which is one of the longest among all living creatures. During this time a person learns languages, science, social behavior and his civic responsibility in a community. Behavioral scientists are baffled by the question whether it is possible to gain all this knowledge if it is not encoded in the DNA of a person. Some scientists argue that the brain as an organ is the repository of all information and intellect. If it is true, then hypothetically a chimpanzee with an implanted human brain should exhibit same ingenuity and creativity as men. We don't know the answer to this riddle yet, but it is known that all newborn children have the capability to learn and acquire new information throughout their lifetime.

In the story of Adam, it is advised by the Quran that there is an afterlife in which a person will be judged for his conduct on earth. In this scenario once a person achieves adulthood, they need spiritual guidance to connect with God as well as to learn about a moral standard through which salvation could be achieved in the afterlife. In religious books, including Quran, there are stories of Prophets and revelation of scriptures given to various civilizations throughout ages to inform them about oneness of God and standards of a moral conduct as member of a community.

This effort to attain enlightenment is not an easy path. Success at this effort is the interplay of three factors that is depth of a personal quest, a benchmark or a message, and spiritual guides that can help. The last two are different in each religion. For Jews these were example of Prophet Moses (RATA) and the Torah. For Christians it is the Bible and Prophet Essa (RATA) (Jesus Christ). For Muslims it is the Quran and Prophet Mohammad (PBUH).

In this context challenge for Muslims is to understand meanings and teachings of the Quran to implement it in their lives. The Quran as a divine revelation which is preserved through centuries is guidance for all ages and times. This means that research to understand its message should be conducted on a continuous basis. It is important because as human knowledge evolves new discoveries are made in science, technology, the human psyche and anthropology.

Muslims hold Quran as a sacred book, but this deference to the book should not put a limit on them to conduct research on it. There is scarcity of Islamic think tanks that are staffed with scholars who have a holistic academic background rather than trained in just the narrow science of Sharia or sacred law. There were individual efforts over centuries to provide new insight into the teachings of Islam. But it may be more effective to organize institutionalized research to produce books that could inform people about the message of the Quran to address political, economic, and social issues prevalent at the time.

It is ironic that there is more research done on the Quran in West than among Muslims. These largely Christian scholars are not approaching

Quran as a divine book to adopt it in their societies but rather to be able to have better understanding of Muslims societies. Research published from these efforts is more useful for Western policy makers and planners than for Muslims who are looking for guidance in incorporating it in their lives. Research efforts sponsored by Abbasid Caliphs (circa 950-1250) still dominate Sharia law taught in Muslim Seminaries to train Imams and Muftis. This backward-looking approach creates an unbridgeable gulf with contemporary period producing misconceptions among Muslims to tackle issues of 21st century. Fatwas, religious edicts, issued by Muftis to address concerns like test tube babies or women photographs on passports in the light of 10th century sharia law is creating an impression that Islam is faith of the past rather than of the present and future.

For non-Muslims the Quran may be a book of wisdom but for Muslims it has in its instructions a method to lead a pious and balanced way of life. This means that understanding its message is imperative for all believers. Here is what the Quran says about understanding its message:

(Verse 25.030) Then the Messenger will say: "O my Lord! Truly my people took this Qur'an for just foolish nonsense."

(Verse 31.021) When they are told to follow the (Revelation) that Allah has sent down, they say: "Nay, we shall follow the ways that we found our fathers (following). "What! even if it is Satan beckoning them to the Penalty of the (Blazing) Fire?

(Verse 38.029) (Here is) a Book which We have sent down unto thee, full of blessings, that they may mediate on its Signs, and that men of understanding may receive admonition.

(Verse 39.018) Those who listen to the Word, and follow the best (meaning) in it: those are the ones whom Allah has guided, and those are the ones endued with understanding.

(Verse 43.078) Verily We have brought the Truth to you: but most of you have a hatred for Truth.

(Verse 54.017) And We have indeed made the Qur'an easy to understand and remember: then is there any that will receive admonition?

From these verses it is important to elaborate a few points that are significant in the context of this book. Quran is emphasizing in many verses that it is incumbent upon men of understanding to contemplate on its signs. In a way it means that those who attain a certain level of wisdom have a higher responsibility to comprehend the message of the Quran.

Why is that? It has a social aspect to it. In usual circumstances people with higher education have a more developed intellect than those who did not have that good fortune. This education provides them with access to economic and social resources. When these empowered people make an effort to understand the message of the Quran, they will be able to convey it to others that may not have opportunities available for it. The second aspect of this is presented in verse 31.021 that it is incumbent on every Muslim to strive in understanding message of Islam through study of the Quran. Unlike Christianity, in Islam there is no designated authority to interpret religious percepts. When a child is born in a Muslim family it does not automatically means he/she will get a good understanding of their faith. Rather they have to make their individual efforts to acquire faith through a rational journey. Salvation in the hereafter is contingent on getting it right when a person had an opportunity during their life on earth.

There are three levels of understanding the Quran which are through educating children, improving understanding of adults, and group under-standing through preaching in Mosques.

As parents when it comes to selecting a school for scientific and social education of our children, we perform extensive due diligence. When choosing a teacher for religious education we select without conducting an in-depth screening of qualifications of potential tutors. We emphasize learning recitation of the Arabic Quran which is important for performing prayers. On the other hand, minimal efforts are made to learn its message by encouraging children to read translation of the Quran in local languages. This failure to inform a child to have a better understanding of religion has a substantial impact on our communities and produces deeply ingrained misconceptions about faith.

A similar lack of interest in religion is exhibited in our adult life. If we take account of our weekly activities, there is hardly any time allocated to reflect on the teachings of the Quran to attain a higher understanding of it. An effective method to learn the Quran is the formation of study groups. There is no hard and fast rule about formation of these study groups but following approach can be more effective:

1. The group should have diversity in terms of level of education, social backgrounds, ages, racial affiliations and sectarian adherence.
2. Discussions should not have preset boundaries in terms of asking questions. Group members should refrain from judging the intention or motivation of the questioner.
3. No question or issue raised should be discarded without giving it due thought and deliberations.
4. Each member of the group should be assigned verses to prepare for these sessions. The objective is to encourage wider participation in leading discussions and prevent domination by one person or a group of people.
5. A creditable translation of the Quran should be used for discussions along with recitation of verses in Arabic. English translations by Abdullah Yusuf Ali, Muhammad Pickthall, and Syed Abul A'la Maududi are considered good because of its simple language.
6. To understand the finer points of Arabic language it is beneficial if the study group has at least one person that has in- depth knowledge of it. This will enable the group to avoid ambiguity arising from translation of a complex word.
7. The Quran was revealed at a particular time and space, so its verses have certain culture and style that was prevalent in that society, but its message is independent of time and space. To understand historical background of verses it may be beneficial to include a moderator who has knowledge of Islamic history and revelation.
8. Success of Quran study group will depend on participation of each member which is hard in a very large group. A group of between 15-20 members may be sufficient.

Most widely used medium to understand the Quran is attending Friday sermons delivered in local mosques. The question we have to explore is whether our mosques are centers of spiritual learning or not? Social decay of Muslim societies could be attributed to failure of our mosques to educate and inform people. Most critical area in which we are failing is selection of our mosque Imams. As individuals we finance mosque through our donations and those who are more active become board members as well. Mosque management boards should conduct extensive search for selecting an Imam. Some important qualifications an Imam should be knowledge of Islamic history, Arabic language, Fiqah, comparison of Islam with other religions of the book, knowledge of contemporary sciences and good grasp of tradition of Prophet Mohammad (PBUH). Mosque board members should look at the curriculum of madrassas, religious seminaries, from which an Imam has graduated to have an appraisal of capabilities of applicants. Many Universities in Muslim and Western countries have departments of Islamic studies. Graduates from these universities should be given an opportunity to become Imams in mosques. This will force traditional Islamic seminaries to reform their curriculum and make it more in line with 21st century requirements.

Once an Imam is hired it is the responsibility of congregants to set the level of expectations from them. Many Muslims are highly educated and achieved PhD and Masters in their respective fields. It defies all logic that these highly educated individuals give a nod of approval to a sermon in which an Imam has clearly misrepresented the teachings of the Quran. It is either that they are not aware of it or do not take enough interest to intervene. It is not the fault of Imams if they fail but all of us as a community because we have not imposed higher standards. Nowadays many people have smart phones in which mobile versions of the Quran translations can be downloaded. Congregants should make it a condition that quotation of the Quranic verse in a Friday sermon should include reference to its chapter and verse number. This way if interpretations do not make sense to listeners, they can refer to translations and have discussions with their Imam after sermon. God expects from us that we will not be passive listeners but active participants. Interactive discourse during delivery of sermon is not permitted in the tradition but our post sermon discussions will force Imams to prepare better.

YouTube.com, Facebook.com and social media are full of videos where some prominent scholars are misquoting from the Quran and narrating events that are fictional than real. The Quran talks about consequences of a preacher's interpreting truth in a twisted way. It is hard to question someone's intention as only God knows the unknown. But there is a way to test the effects of an interpretation. If a preacher is dividing Ummah and producing bloodshed among Muslims, then it is important to closely scrutinize their message to stop them from propagating further.

Many newspapers and magazine quote verses from the Quran when talking about Islamic teachings. In some instances, it could have an adverse effect. First, a verse quoted out of context can have a totally different meaning than what is intended. Second, in some cases wrong translation or verse number is quoted. It is required from conscientious Muslims especially those who are engaged in preaching and propagating Islam to help in preventing these occurrences. Letters should be written to publications to retract those articles where verses are quoted out of context and corrections should be published in case wrong translation was used. These steps will go a long way in improving perception of Islam and promote its message of peace through justice.

Despite negative publicity of Islam and the Quran in Western media, most converts mention the Quran as their source of getting enlightenment. It is something to think about. During first few centuries of advent of Islam, it was character of Muslims that became a prime source of conversions while in 21st century these personal examples are scarce.

One common observation made by new converts is that Muslims are too focused on cultural and symbolic aspect of religion than its spiritual content and exercising it in their life. For instance, it should be more important to be truthful than measuring the size of a person's beard. Or standing up to oppose oppression than wearing pants with bottoms above ankles. These symbols are more reflective of culture and should be a matter of personal choice rather than incorporating it as mandatory part of religion. Similarly, it is the message which is sacred not that the Arabic language in itself is sacrosanct.

Recitation of Arabic verses is mandatory in religious rites and prayers. But God taught us other languages as well to empower us to understand the Quran in our native language especially when translations are readily available. Ignoring this important responsibility would mean that we cannot implement teachings of the Quran in our lives, which should be a concern for all of us. Muslims tend to become emotional about their faith and endow superlative in presenting it. But if this superiority of faith is not reflected in Muslim societies, then it is a hollow claim. Only a collective effort can help us resolve this paradox.

This compilation of verses is a humble effort to understand the message of the Quran with a focus on its social relevance. It is important to note that individual verses can never be an alternative to reading the Quran in entirety. The idea of this compilation is that if a verse is presented about business transaction or dealing with non-Muslims then it is expected that a reader will read the whole chapter to understand context of the given reference. Here is what the Quran says about this responsibility:

(Verse 29.002) Do men think that they will be left alone on saying, "We believe", and that they will not be tested?

(Verse 33.008) That (Allah) may question the (custodians) of Truth concerning the Truth they (were charged with): And He has prepared for the Unbelievers a grievous Penalty.

This compilation has seven sections each focusing on a particular aspect of faith and social life. Each section has multiple topics corresponding to the theme of a section. Verse numbers are provided to enable readers to refer to the Quran. For instance, Verse 6.025 would mean Chapter 6 (called Sura in Arabic) of the Quran and Verse 25 in that chapter. Verses in each topic are presented in an ascending number order. The verses that are in a sequence are grouped together to convey the whole message. This compilation uses the translation of Abdullah Yusuf Ali. Cover picture is minaret of 900 years old Sidi Boumediene Mosque in Tlemcen, Algeria. The picture was taken by my wife Dr. Zoulikha Mouffak during our trip to Algeria.

I would like to acknowledge Seyed Ali Ghazvini, Director of Islamic Cultural Center Fresno (ICCF) for providing guidance in understanding the Quran. He was gracefully patient to answer my never-ending array of questions. This compilation was reviewed by my dear friend Muhammad Haroon Ilyas to ensure there were no errors in verse numbers and their corresponding content.

Errors and omissions are intrinsic to being human. I seek forgiveness from God for an unintentional and unintended error.

In the end, I would like you to join me in praying that God gives us knowledge and wisdom to understand the true message of the Quran and practice it in our lives. I would also like you to pray for the departed soul of Abdullah Yusuf Ali whose translation of the Quran has been a source of understanding for many Muslims and non-Muslims alike. May God bless his soul and raise his ranks in the heaven. Amen.

Abdul Quayyum Khan Kundi
Clovis, California
June 8, 2012

I

Foundations of Faith

Significance of Quran

(Verse 2.185) Ramadhan is the (month) in which was sent down the Qur'an, as a guide to mankind, also clear (Signs) for guidance and judgment (Between right and wrong). So every one of you who is present (at his home) during that month should spend it in fasting, but if any one is ill, or on a journey, the prescribed period (Should be made up) by days later. Allah intends every facility for you; He does not want to put to difficulties. (He wants you) to complete the prescribed period, and to glorify Him in that He has guided you; and perchance ye shall be grateful.

(Verse 3.003) It is He Who sent down to thee (step by step), in truth, the Book, confirming what went before it; and He sent down the Law (of Moses) and the Gospel (of Jesus) before this, as a guide to mankind, and He sent down the criterion (of judgment between right and wrong).

(Verse 3.007) He it is Who has sent down to thee the Book: In it are verses basic or fundamental (of established meaning); they are the foundation of the Book: others are allegorical. But those in whose hearts is perversity follow the part thereof that is allegorical, seeking discord, and searching for its hidden meanings, but no one knows its hidden meanings except Allah. And those who are firmly grounded in knowledge say: "We believe in the Book; the whole of it is from our Lord:" and none will grasp the Message except men of understanding.

(Verse 3.044) This is part of the tidings of the things unseen, which We reveal unto thee (O Messenger!) by inspiration: Thou wast not with them when they cast lots with arrows, as to which of them should be charged with the care of Mary: Nor wast thou with them when they disputed (the point).

(Verse 3.050) "'(I have come to you), to attest the Law which was before me. And to make lawful to you part of what was (Before) forbidden to you; I have come to you with a Sign from your Lord. So fear Allah, and obey me.

(Verse 4.113) But for the Grace of Allah to thee and his Mercy, a party of them would certainly have plotted to lead thee astray. But (in fact) they will only lead their own souls astray, and to thee they can do no harm in the least. For Allah hath sent down to thee the Book and wisdom and taught thee what thou Knewest not (before): And great is the Grace of Allah unto thee.

(Verse 4.136) O ye who believe! Believe in Allah and His Messenger, and the scripture which He hath sent to His Messenger and the scripture which He sent to those before (him). Any who denieth Allah, His angels, His Books, His Messengers, and the Day of Judgment, hath gone far, far astray.

(Verse 4.163) We have sent thee inspiration, as We sent it to Noah and the Messengers after him: we sent inspiration to Abraham, Isma'il, Isaac, Jacob and the Tribes, to Jesus, Job, Jonah, Aaron, and Solomon, and to David We gave the Psalms.

(Verse 4.166) But Allah beareth witness that what He hath sent unto thee He hath sent from His (own) knowledge, and the angels bear witness: But enough is Allah for a witness.

(Verse 4.174) O mankind! Verily there hath come to you a convincing proof from your Lord: For We have sent unto you a light (that is) manifest.

(Verse 5.015) O people of the Book! There hath come to you our Messenger, revealing to you much that ye used to hide in the Book, and passing over much (that is now unnecessary): There hath come to you from Allah a (new) light and a perspicuous Book, -

(Verse 5.059) Say: "O people of the Book! Do ye disapprove of us for no other reason than that we believe in Allah, and the revelation that hath come to us and that which came before (us), and (perhaps) that most of you are rebellious and disobedient?"

(Verse 5.066) If only they had stood fast by the Law, the Gospel, and all the revelation that was sent to them from their Lord, they would have enjoyed happiness from every side. There is from among them a party on the right course: but many of them follow a course that is evil. (Verse 5.067) O

Messenger! Proclaim the (message) which hath been sent to thee from thy Lord. If thou didst not, thou wouldst not have fulfilled and proclaimed His mission. And Allah will defend thee from men (who mean mischief). For Allah guideth not those who reject Faith. (Verse 5.068) Say: "O People of the Book! ye have no ground to stand upon unless ye stand fast by the Law, the Gospel, and all the revelation that has come to you from your Lord." It is the revelation that cometh to thee from thy Lord, that increaseth in most of them their obstinate rebellion and blasphemy. But sorrow thou not over (these) people without Faith. (Verse 5.069) Those who believe (in the Qur'an), those who follow the Jewish (scriptures), and the Sabians and the Christians,- any who believe in Allah and the Last Day, and work righteousness,- on them shall be no fear, nor shall they grieve.

(Verse 5.101) O ye who believe! Ask not questions about things which, if made plain to you, may cause you trouble. But if ye ask about things when the Qur'an is being revealed, they will be made plain to you, Allah will forgive those: for Allah is Oft-forgiving, Most Forbearing. (Verse 5.102) Some people before you did ask such questions, and on that account lost their faith.

(Verse 6.019) Say: "What thing is most weighty in evidence?" Say: "Allah is witness between me and you; This Qur'an hath been revealed to me by inspiration, that I may warn you and all whom it reaches. Can ye possibly bear witness that besides Allah there is another Allah?" Say: "Nay! I cannot bear witness!" Say: "But in truth He is the one Allah, and I truly am innocent of (your blasphemy of) joining others with Him."

(Verse 6.092) And this is a Book which We have sent down, bringing blessings, and confirming (the revelations) which came before it: that thou mayest warn the mother of cities and all around her. Those who believe in the Hereafter believe in this (Book), and they are constant in guarding their prayers.

(Verse 6.106) Follow what thou art taught by inspiration from thy Lord: there is no god but He: and turn aside from those who join gods with Allah.

(Verse 6.114) Say: "Shall I seek for judge other than Allah? - when He it is Who hath sent unto you the Book, explained in detail." They know full well, to whom We have given the Book, that it hath been sent down from thy Lord in truth. Never be then of those who doubt.

(Verse 6.155) And this is a Book which We have revealed as a blessing: so follow it and be righteous, that ye may receive mercy: (Verse 6.156) Lest ye should say: "The Book was sent down to two Peoples before us, and for our part, we remained unacquainted with all that they learned by assiduous study:" (Verse 6.157) Or lest ye should say: "If the Book had only been sent down to us, we should have followed its guidance better than they." Now then hath come unto you a clear (sign) from your Lord,- and a guide and a mercy: then who could do more wrong than one who rejecteth Allah's signs, and turneth away therefrom? In good time shall We requite those who turn away from Our signs, with a dreadful penalty, for their turning away.

(Verse 7.002) A Book revealed unto thee,- So let thy heart be oppressed no more by any difficulty on that account,- that with it thou mightest warn (the erring) and teach the Believers). (Verse 7.003) Follow (O men!) the revelation given unto you from your Lord, and follow not, as friends, or protectors, other than Him. Little it is ye remember of admonition.

(Verse 7.052) For We had certainly sent unto them a Book, based on knowledge, which We explained in detail,- a guide and a mercy to all who believe.

(Verse 7.196) "For my Protector is Allah, Who revealed the Book (from time to time), and He will choose and befriend the righteous."

(Verse 7.204) When the Qur'an is read, listen to it with attention, and hold your peace: that ye may receive Mercy.

(Verse 9.124) Whenever there cometh down a sura, some of them say: "Which of you has had His faith increased by it?" Yea, those who believe,- their faith is increased and they do rejoice. (Verse 9.125) But those in whose hearts is a disease,- it will add doubt to their doubt, and they will die in a state of Unbelief.

(Verse 9.127) Whenever there cometh down a Sura, they look at each other, (saying), "Doth anyone see you?" Then they turn aside: Allah hath turned their hearts (from the light); for they are a people that understand not.

(Verse 10.037) This Qur'an is not such as can be produced by other than

Allah; on the contrary it is a confirmation of (revelations) that went before it, and a fuller explanation of the Book - wherein there is no doubt - from the Lord of the worlds.

(Verse 10.057) O mankind! There hath come to you a direction from your Lord and a healing for the (diseases) in your hearts,- and for those who believe, a guidance and a Mercy.

(Verse 10.094) If thou wert in doubt as to what We have revealed unto thee, then ask those who have been reading the Book from before thee: the Truth hath indeed come to thee from thy Lord: so be in no wise of those in doubt.

(Verse 10.108) Say: "O ye men! Now Truth hath reached you from your Lord! Those who receive guidance, do so for the good of their own souls; those who stray, do so to their own loss: and I am not (set) over you to arrange your affairs.

(Verse 11.001) A. L. R. (This is) a Book, with verses basic or fundamental (of established meaning), further explained in detail,- from One Who is Wise and Well-acquainted (with all things): (Verse 11.002) (It teacheth) that ye should worship none but Allah. (Say): "Verily I am (sent) unto you from Him to warn and to bring glad tidings: (Verse 11.003) "(And to preach thus), 'Seek ye the forgiveness of your Lord, and turn to Him in repentance; that He may grant you enjoyment, good (and true), for a term appointed, and bestow His abounding grace on all who abound in merit! But if ye turn away, then I fear for you the penalty of a great day: (Verse 11.004) 'To Allah is your return, and He hath power over all things.'"

(Verse 11.012) Perchance thou mayest (feel the inclination) to give up a part of what is revealed unto thee, and thy heart feeleth straitened lest they say, "Why is not a treasure sent down unto him, or why does not an angel come down with him?" But thou art there only to warn! It is Allah that arrangeth all affairs! (Verse 11.013) Or they may say, "He forged it," Say, "Bring ye then ten suras forged, like unto it, and call (to your aid) whomsoever ye can, other than Allah!- If ye speak the truth! (Verse 11.014) "If then they (your false gods) answer not your (call), know ye that this revelation is sent down (replete) with the knowledge of Allah, and that there is no god but He! will ye even then submit (to Islam)?"

(Verse 12.001) A.L.R. These are the symbols (or Verses) of the perspicuous Book. (Verse 12.002) We have sent it down as an Arabic Qur'an, in order that ye may learn wisdom.

(Verse 13.001) A. L. M. R. These are the signs (or verses) of the Book: that which hath been revealed unto thee from thy Lord is the Truth; but most men believe not.

(Verse 13.019) Is then one who doth know that that which hath been revealed unto thee from thy Lord is the Truth, like one who is blind? It is those who are endued with understanding that receive admonition;-

(Verse 13.031) If there were a Qur'an with which mountains were moved, or the earth were cloven asunder, or the dead were made to speak, (this would be the one!) But, truly, the command is with Allah in all things! Do not the Believers know, that, had Allah (so) willed, He could have guided all mankind (to the right)? But the Unbelievers,- never will disaster cease to seize them for their (ill) deeds, or to settle close to their homes, until the promise of Allah come to pass, for, verily, Allah will not fail in His promise.

(Verse 13.036) Those to whom We have given the Book rejoice at what hath been revealed unto thee: but there are among the clans those who reject a part thereof. Say: "I am commanded to worship Allah, and not to join partners with Him. Unto Him do I call, and unto Him is my return." (Verse 13.037) Thus have We revealed it to be a judgment of authority in Arabic. Wert thou to follow their (vain) desires after the knowledge which hath reached thee, then wouldst thou find neither protector nor defender against Allah. (Verse 13.038) We did send messengers before thee, and appointed for them wives and children: and it was never the part of a messenger to bring a sign except as Allah permitted (or commanded). For each period is a Book (revealed). (Verse 13.039) Allah doth blot out or confirm what He pleaseth: with Him is the Mother of the Book.

(Verse 14.001) A. L. R. A Book which We have revealed unto thee, in order that thou mightest lead mankind out of the depths of darkness into light - by the leave of their Lord - to the Way of (Him) the Exalted in power, worthy of all praise!-

(Verse 15.001) A. L. R. These are the Ayats of Revelation,- of a Qur'an that makes things clear.

(Verse 15.009) We have, without doubt, sent down the Message; and We will assuredly guard it (from corruption).

(Verse 15.087) And We have bestowed upon thee the Seven Oft-repeated (verses) and the Grand Qur'an.

(Verse 16.044) (We sent them) with Clear Signs and Books of dark prophecies; and We have sent down unto thee (also) the Message; that thou mayest explain clearly to men what is sent for them, and that they may give thought.

(Verse 16.064) And We sent down the Book to thee for the express purpose, that thou shouldst make clear to them those things in which they differ, and that it should be a guide and a mercy to those who believe.

(Verse 16.089) One day We shall raise from all Peoples a witness against them, from amongst themselves: and We shall bring thee as a witness against these (thy people): and We have sent down to thee the Book explaining all things, a Guide, a Mercy, and Glad Tidings to Muslims.

(Verse 16.098) When thou dost read the Qur'an, seek Allah's protection from Satan the rejected one. (Verse 16.099) No authority has he over those who believe and put their trust in their Lord.

(Verse 16.101) When We substitute one revelation for another,- and Allah knows best what He reveals (in stages),- they say, "Thou art but a forger": but most of them understand not. (Verse 16.102) Say, the Holy Spirit has brought the revelation from thy Lord in Truth, in order to strengthen those who believe, and as a Guide and Glad Tidings to Muslims.

(Verse 17.009) Verily this Qur'an doth guide to that which is most right (or stable), and giveth the Glad Tidings to the Believers who work deeds of righteousness, that they shall have a magnificent reward;

(Verse 17.041) We have explained (things) in various (ways) in this Qur'an, in order that they may receive admonition, but it only increases their flight (from the Truth)!

(Verse 17.045) When thou dost recite the Qur'an, We put, between thee and those who believe not in the Hereafter, a veil invisible:

(Verse 17.082) We send down (stage by stage) in the Qur'an that which is a healing and a mercy to those who believe: to the unjust it causes nothing but loss after loss.

(Verse 17.088) Say: "If the whole of mankind and Jinns were to gather together to produce the like of this Qur'an, they could not produce the like thereof, even if they backed up each other with help and support." (Verse 17.089) And We have explained to man, in this Qur'an, every kind of similitude: yet the greater part of men refuse (to receive it) except with ingratitude!

(Verse 17.105) We sent down the (Qur'an) in Truth, and in Truth has it descended: and We sent thee but to give Glad Tidings and to warn (sinners). (Verse 17.106) (It is) a Qur'an which We have divided (into parts from time to time), in order that thou mightest recite it to men at intervals: We have revealed it by stages.

(Verse 18.001) Praise be to Allah, Who hath sent to His Servant the Book, and hath allowed therein no Crookedness: (Verse 18.002) (He hath made it) Straight (and Clear) in order that He may warn (the godless) of a terrible Punishment from Him, and that He may give Glad Tidings to the Believers who work righteousness deeds, that they shall have a goodly Reward.

(Verse 18.027) And recite (and teach) what has been revealed to thee of the Book of thy Lord: none can change His Words, and none wilt thou find as a refuge other than Him.

(Verse 18.054) We have explained in detail in this Qur'an, for the benefit of mankind, every kind of similitude: but man is, in most things, contentious. (Verse 18.055) And what is there to keep back men from believing, now that Guidance has come to them, nor from praying for forgiveness from their Lord, but that (they ask that) the ways of the ancients be repeated with them, or the Wrath be brought to them face to face?

(Verse 19.097) So have We made the (Qur'an) easy in thine own tongue, that with it thou mayest give Glad Tidings to the righteous, and warnings to people given to contention.

(Verse 20.002) We have not sent down the Qur'an to thee to be (an occasion) for thy distress, (Verse 20.003) But only as an admonition to those who fear (Allah),- (Verse 20.004) A revelation from Him Who created the earth and the heavens on high.

(Verse 20.113) Thus have We sent this down - an Arabic Qur'an - and explained therein in detail some of the warnings, in order that they may fear Allah, or that it may cause their remembrance (of Him).

(Verse 21.010) We have revealed for you (O men!) a book in which is a Message for you: will ye not then understand?

(Verse 21.050) And this is a blessed Message which We have sent down: will ye then reject it?

(Verse 21.106) Verily in this (Qur'an) is a Message for people who would (truly) worship Allah.

(Verse 22.017) Those who believe (in the Qur'an), those who follow the Jewish (scriptures), and the Sabians, Christians, Magians, and Polytheists,- Allah will judge between them on the Day of Judgment: for Allah is witness of all things.

(Verse 22.054) And that those on whom knowledge has been bestowed may learn that the (Qur'an) is the Truth from thy Lord, and that they may believe therein, and their hearts may be made humbly (open) to it: for verily Allah is the Guide of those who believe, to the Straight Way.

(Verse 23.068) Do they not ponder over the Word (of Allah), or has anything (new) come to them that did not come to their fathers of old?

(Verse 25.001) Blessed is He who sent down the criterion to His servant, that it may be an admonition to all creatures;-

(Verse 25.006) Say: "The (Qur'an) was sent down by Him who knows the mystery (that is) in the heavens and the earth: verily He is Oft-Forgiving, Most Merciful."

(Verse 25.030) Then the Messenger will say: "O my Lord! Truly my people took this Qur'an for just foolish nonsense."

(Verse 25.032) Those who reject Faith say: "Why is not the Qur'an revealed to him all at once? Thus (is it revealed), that We may strengthen thy heart thereby, and We have rehearsed it to thee in slow, well-arranged stages, gradually.

(Verse 26.002) These are verses of the Book that makes (things) clear.

(Verse 26.192) Verily this is a Revelation from the Lord of the Worlds:

(Verse 26.193) With it came down the spirit of Faith and Truth- (Verse 26.194) To thy heart and mind, that thou mayest admonish.

(Verse 26.210) No evil ones have brought down this (Revelation): (Verse 26.211) It would neither suit them nor would they be able (to produce it). (Verse 26.212) Indeed they have been removed far from even (a chance of) hearing it.

(Verse 27.001) These are verses of the Qur'an,-a book that makes (things) clear; (Verse 27.002) A guide: and glad tidings for the believers,-

(Verse 27.006) As to thee, the Qur'an is bestowed upon thee from the presence of one who is wise and all-knowing.

(Verse 28.02) These are Verses of the Book that makes (things) clear.

(Verse 28.085) Verily He Who ordained the Qur'an for thee, will bring thee back to the Place of Return. Say: "My Lord knows best who it is that brings true guidance, and who is in manifest error." (Verse 28.086) And thou hadst not expected that the Book would be sent to thee except as a Mercy from thy Lord: Therefore lend not thou support in any way to those who reject (Allah's Message). (Verse 28.087) And let nothing keep thee back from the Signs of Allah after they have been revealed to thee: and invite (men) to thy Lord, and be not of the company of those who join gods with Allah.

(Verse 29.047) And thus (it is) that We have sent down the Book to thee. So the People of the Book believe therein, as also do some of these (pagan Arabs): and none but Unbelievers reject our signs. (Verse 29.048) And thou wast not (able) to recite a Book before this (Book came), nor art thou (able) to transcribe it with thy right hand: In that case, indeed, would the talkers of vanities have doubted. (Verse 29.049) Nay, here are Signs self-evident in the hearts of those endowed with knowledge: and none but the unjust reject Our Signs. (Verse 29.050) Ye they say: "Why are not Signs sent down to him from his Lord?" Say: "The signs are indeed with Allah: and I am indeed a clear Warner." (Verse 29.051) And is it not enough for them that we have sent down to thee the Book which is rehearsed to them? Verily, in it is Mercy and a Reminder to those who believe.

(Verse 30.058) Verily We have propounded for men, in this Qur'an every kind of Parable: But if thou bring to them any Sign, the Unbelievers are sure to say, "Ye do nothing but talk vanities."

(Verse 31.002) These are Verses of the Wise Book,- (Verse 31.003) A Guide and a Mercy to the Doers of Good,-

(Verse 32.002) (This is) the Revelation of the Book in which there is no doubt,- from the Lord of the Worlds. (Verse 32.003) Or do they say, "He has forged it"? Nay, it is the Truth from thy Lord, that thou mayest admonish a people to whom no warner has come before thee: in order that they may receive guidance.

(Verse 33.002) But follow that which comes to thee by inspiration from thy Lord: for Allah is well acquainted with (all) that ye do.

(Verse 34.006) And those to whom knowledge has come see that the (Revelation) sent down to thee from thy Lord - that is the Truth, and that it guides to the Path of the Exalted (in might), Worthy of all praise.

(Verse 34.049) Say: "The Truth has arrived, and Falsehood neither creates anything new, nor restores anything." (Verse 34.050) Say: "If I am astray, I only stray to the loss of my own soul: but if I receive guidance, it is because of the inspiration of my Lord to me: it is He Who hears all things, and is (ever) near."

(Verse 35.031) That which We have revealed to thee of the Book is the Truth,- confirming what was (revealed) before it: for Allah is assuredly- with respect to His Servants - well acquainted and Fully Observant. (Verse 35.032) Then We have given the Book for inheritance to such of Our Servants as We have chosen: but there are among them some who wrong their own souls; some who follow a middle course; and some who are, by Allah's leave, foremost in good deeds; that is the highest Grace.

(Verse 36.002) By the Qur'an, full of Wisdom,-

(Verse 36.005) It is a Revelation sent down by (Him), the Exalted in Might, Most Merciful.

(Verse 36.069) We have not instructed the (Prophet) in Poetry, nor is it meet for him: this is no less than a Message and a Qur'an making things clear: (Verse 36.070) That it may give admonition to any (who are) alive, and that the charge may be proved against those who reject (Truth).

(Verse 37.170) But (now that the Qur'an has come), they reject it: But soon will they know!

(Verse 38.001) Sad: By the Qur'an, Full of Admonition: (This is the Truth).

(Verse 38.029) (Here is) a Book which We have sent down unto thee, full of blessings, that they may mediate on its Signs, and that men of understanding may receive admonition.

(Verse 38.067) Say: "That is a Message Supreme (above all),- (Verse 38.068) "From which ye do turn away! (Verse 38.069) "No knowledge have I of the Chiefs on high, when they discuss (matters) among themselves. (Verse 38.070) 'Only this has been revealed to me: that I am to give warning plainly and publicly."

(Verse 39.001) The revelation of this Book is from Allah, the Exalted in Power, full of Wisdom. (Verse 39.002) Verily it is We Who have revealed the Book to thee in Truth: so serve Allah, offering Him sincere devotion.

(Verse 39.018) Those who listen to the Word, and follow the best (meaning) in it: those are the ones whom Allah has guided, and those are the ones endued with understanding.

(Verse 39.023) Allah has revealed (from time to time) the most beautiful Message in the form of a Book, consistent with itself, (yet) repeating (its teaching in various aspects): the skins of those who fear their Lord tremble thereat; then their skins and their hearts do soften to the celebration of Allah's praises. Such is the guidance of Allah: He guides therewith whom He pleases, but such as Allah leaves to stray, can have none to guide.

(Verse 39.027) We have put forth for men, in this Qur'an every kind of Parable, in order that they may receive admonition. (Verse 39.028) (It is) a Qur'an in Arabic, without any crookedness (therein): in order that they may guard against Evil.

(Verse 40.002) The revelation of this Book is from Allah, Exalted in Power, Full of Knowledge,-

(Verse 40.070) Those who reject the Book and the (revelations) with which We sent our messengers: but soon shall they know,-

(Verse 41.002) A Revelation from (Allah), Most Gracious, Most Merciful;- (Verse 41.003) A Book, whereof the verses are explained in detail;- a Qur'an in Arabic, for people who understand;- (Verse 41.004) Giving good news and admonition: yet most of them turn away, and so they hear not.

(Verse 41.041) Those who reject the Message when it comes to them (are not hidden from Us). And indeed it is a Book of exalted power. (Verse 41.042) No falsehood can approach it from before or behind it: It is sent down by One Full of Wisdom, Worthy of all Praise.

(Verse 41.044) Had We sent this as a Qur'an (in the language) other than Arabic, they would have said: "Why are not its verses explained in detail? What! (a Book) not in Arabic and (a Messenger an Arab?" Say: "It is a Guide and a Healing to those who believe; and for those who believe not, there is a deafness in their ears, and it is blindness in their (eyes): They are (as it were) being called from a place far distant!"

(Verse 41.045) We certainly gave Moses the Book aforetime: but disputes arose therein. Had it not been for a Word that went forth before from thy Lord, (their differences) would have been settled between them: but they remained in suspicious disquieting doubt thereon.

(Verse 41.052) Say: "See ye if the (Revelation) is (really) from Allah, and yet do ye reject it? Who is more astray than one who is in a schism far (from any purpose)?"

(Verse 42.007) Thus have We sent by inspiration to thee an Arabic Qur'an: that thou mayest warn the Mother of Cities and all around her,- and warn (them) of the Day of Assembly, of which there is no doubt: (when) some will be in the Garden, and some in the Blazing Fire.

(Verse 42.017) It is Allah Who has sent down the Book in Truth, and the Balance (by which to weigh conduct). And what will make thee realize that perhaps the Hour is close at hand?

(Verse 42.052) And thus have We, by Our Command, sent inspiration to thee: thou knewest not (before) what was Revelation, and what was Faith; but We have made the (Qur'an) a Light, wherewith We guide such of Our servants as We will; and verily thou dost guide (men) to the Straight Way,-

(Verse 43.002) By the Book that makes things clear,- (Verse 43.003) We have made it a Qur'an in Arabic, that ye may be able to understand (and learn wisdom). (Verse 43.004) And verily, it is in the Mother of the Book, in Our Presence, high (in dignity), full of wisdom. (Verse 43.005) Shall We then take away the Message from you and repel (you), for that ye are a people transgressing beyond bounds?

(Verse 43.043) So hold thou fast to the Revelation sent down to thee; verily thou art on a Straight Way. (Verse 43.044) The (Qur'an) is indeed the message, for thee and for thy people; and soon shall ye (all) be brought to account.

(Verse 43.078) Verily We have brought the Truth to you: but most of you have a hatred for Truth.

(Verse 44.002) By the Book that makes things clear;- (Verse 44.003) We sent it down during a Blessed Night: for We (ever) wish to warn (against Evil). (Verse 44.004) In the (Night) is made distinct every affair of wisdom, (Verse 44.005) By command, from Our Presence. For We (ever) send (revelations), (Verse 44.006) As Mercy from thy Lord: for He hears and knows (all things);

(Verse 44.058) Verily, We have made this (Qur'an) easy, in thy tongue, in order that they may give heed.

(Verse 45.002) The revelation of the Book is from Allah the Exalted in Power, Full of Wisdom.

(Verse 46.002) The Revelation of the Book is from Allah the Exalted in Power, Full of Wisdom.

(Verse 47.002) But those who believe and work deeds of righteousness, and believe in the (Revelation) sent down to Muhammad - for it is the Truth from their Lord,- He will remove from them their ills and improve their condition.

(Verse 54.017) And We have indeed made the Qur'an easy to understand and remember: then is there any that will receive admonition?

(Verse 55.002) It is He Who has taught the Qur'an.

(Verse 56.077) That this is indeed a Qur'an Most Honorable, (Verse 56.078) In Book well-guarded, (Verse 56.079) Which none shall touch but those who are clean: (Verse 56.080) A Revelation from the Lord of the Worlds. (Verse 56.081) Is it such a Message that ye would hold in light esteem? (Verse 56.082) And have ye made it your livelihood that ye should declare it false?

(Verse 59.021) Had We sent down this Qur'an on a mountain, verily, thou wouldst have seen it humble itself and cleave asunder for fear of Allah. Such are the similitudes which We propound to men, that they may reflect.

(Verse 69.040) That this is verily the word of an honored messenger; (Verse 69.041) It is not the word of a poet: little it is ye believe! (Verse 69.042) Nor is it the word of a soothsayer: little admonition it is ye receive. (Verse 69.043) (This is) a Message sent down from the Lord of the Worlds. (Verse 69.044) And if the messenger were to invent any sayings in Our name, (Verse 69.045) We should certainly seize him by his right hand, (Verse 69.046) And We should certainly then cut off the artery of his heart:

(Verse 69.048) But verily this is a Message for the Allah-fearing. (Verse 69.049) And We certainly know that there are amongst you those that reject (it). (Verse 69.050) But truly (Revelation) is a cause of sorrow for the Unbelievers. (Verse 69.051) But verily it is Truth of assured certainty.

(Verse 72.001) Say: It has been revealed to me that a company of jinns listened (to the Quran). They said, 'We have really heard a wonderful Recital! (Verse 72.002) 'It gives guidance to the Right, and we have believed therein: we shall not join (in worship) any (gods) with out Lord.

(Verse 75.016) Move not thy tongue concerning the (Qur'an) to make haste therewith. (Verse 75.017) It is for Us to collect it and to promulgate it: (Verse 75.018) But when We have promulgated it, follow thou its recital (as promulgated): (Verse 75.019) Nay more, it is for Us to explain it (and make it clear):

(Verse 76.023) It is We Who have sent down the Qur'an to thee by stages.

(Verse 80.013) (It is) in Books held (greatly) in honor, (Verse 80.014) Exalted (in dignity), kept pure and holy, (Verse 80.015) (Written) by the hands of scribes- (Verse 80.016) Honorable and Pious and Just.

(Verse 85.021) Nay, this is a Glorious Quran, (Verse 85.022) (Inscribed) in a Tablet Preserved!

(Verse 86.013) Behold this is the Word that distinguishes (Good from Evil): (Verse 86.014) It is not a thing for amusement.

(Verse 87.006) By degrees shall We teach thee to declare (the Message), so thou shalt not forget,

(Verse 87.018) And this is in the Books of the earliest (Revelation),- (Verse 87.019) The Books of Abraham and Moses.

(Verse 97.001) We have indeed revealed this (Message) in the Night of

Power:

Validating Prophet Mohammad (PBUH)

(Verse 3.031) Say: "If ye do love Allah, Follow me: Allah will love you and forgive you your sins: For Allah is Oft-Forgiving, Most Merciful." (Verse 3.032) Say: "Obey Allah and His Messenger": But if they turn back, Allah loveth not those who reject Faith.

(Verse 3.132) And obey Allah and the Messenger; that ye may obtain mercy.

(Verse 3.144) Muhammad is no more than a messenger: many were the messenger that passed away before him. If he died or were slain, will ye then turn back on your heels? If any did turn back on his heels, not the least harm will he do to Allah; but Allah (on the other hand) will swiftly reward those who (serve Him) with gratitude.

(Verse 3.164) Allah did confer a great favor on the believers when He sent among them a messenger from among themselves, rehearsing unto them the Signs of Allah, sanctifying them, and instructing them in Scripture and Wisdom, while, before that, they had been in manifest error.

(Verse 3.179) Allah will not leave the believers in the state in which ye are now, until He separates what is evil from what is good nor will He disclose to you the secrets of the Unseen. But He chooses of His Messengers (For the purpose) whom He pleases. So believe in Allah. And His messengers: And if ye believe and do right, ye have a reward without measure.

(Verse 3.184) Then if they reject thee, so were rejected messengers before thee, who came with Clear Signs, Books of dark prophecies, and the Book of Enlightenment.

(Verse 3.199) And there are, certainly, among the People of the Book, those who believe in Allah, in the revelation to you, and in the revelation to them, bowing in humility to Allah: They will not sell the Signs of Allah for a miserable gain! For them is a reward with their Lord, and Allah is swift in account.

(Verse 4.115) If anyone contends with the Messenger even after guidance has been plainly conveyed to him, and follows a path other than that becoming to men of Faith, We shall leave him in the path he has chosen, and land him in Hell,- what an evil refuge!

(Verse 4.170) O Mankind! The Messenger hath come to you in truth from Allah: believe in him: It is best for you. But if ye reject Faith, to Allah belong all things in the heavens and on earth: And Allah is All-knowing, All-wise.

(Verse 5.019) O People of the Book! Now hath come unto you, making (things) clear unto you, Our Messenger, after the break in (the series of) our messengers, lest ye should say: "There came unto us no bringer of glad tidings and no Warner (from evil)": But now hath come unto you a bringer of glad tidings and a Warner (from evil). And Allah hath power over all things.

(Verse 5.092) Obey Allah, and obey the Messenger, and beware (of evil): if ye do turn back, know ye that it is Our Messenger's duty to proclaim (the message) in the clearest manner.

(Verse 5.099) The Messenger's duty is but to proclaim (the message). But Allah knoweth all that ye reveal and ye conceal.

(Verse 6.034) Rejected were the messengers before thee: with patience and constancy they bore their rejection and their wrongs, until Our aid did reach them: there is none that can alter the words (and decrees) of Allah. Already hast thou received some account of those messengers.

(Verse 6.048) We send the messengers only to give good news and to warn: so those who believe and mend (their lives),- upon them shall be no fear, nor shall they grieve.

(Verse 6.050) Say: "I tell you not that with me are the treasures of Allah, nor do I know what is hidden, nor do I tell you I am an angel. I but follow what is revealed to me." Say: "can the blind be held equal to the seeing?" Will ye then consider not?

(Verse 6.066) But thy people reject this, though it is the truth. Say: "Not mine is the responsibility for arranging your affairs; (Verse 6.067) For every message is a limit of time, and soon shall ye know it."

(Verse 7.157)"Those who follow the messenger, the unlettered Prophet, whom they find mentioned in their own (scriptures),- in the law and the Gospel;- for he commands them what is just and forbids them what is evil; he allows them as lawful what is good (and pure) and prohibits them from what is bad (and impure); He releases them from their heavy burdens and from the yokes that are upon them. So it is those who believe in him, honor him, help him, and follow the light which is sent down with him,- it is they who will prosper." (Verse 7.158) Say: "O men! I am sent unto you all, as the Messenger of Allah, to Whom belongeth the dominion of the heavens and the earth: there is no god but He: it is He That giveth both life and death. So believe in Allah and His Messenger, the Unlettered Prophet, who believeth in Allah and His words: follow him that (so) ye may be guided."

(Verse 7.188) Say: "I have no power over any good or harm to myself except as Allah willeth. If I had knowledge of the unseen, I should have multiplied all good, and no evil should have touched me: I am but a Warner, and a bringer of glad tidings to those who have faith."

(Verse 7.203) If thou bring them not a revelation, they say: "Why hast thou not got it together?" Say: "I but follow what is revealed to me from my Lord: this is (nothing but) lights from your Lord, and Guidance, and mercy, for any who have faith."

(Verse 9.033) It is He Who hath sent His Messenger with guidance and the Religion of Truth, to proclaim it over all religion, even though the Pagans may detest (it).

(Verse 9.061) Among them are men who molest the Prophet and say, "He is (all) ear." Say, "He listens to what is best for you: he believes in Allah, has faith in the Believers, and is a Mercy to those of you who believe." But those who molest the Messenger will have a grievous penalty.

(Verse 9.128) Now hath come unto you a Messenger from amongst yourselves: it grieves him that ye should perish: ardently anxious is he over you: to the Believers is he most kind and merciful. (Verse 9.129) But if they turn away, Say: "Allah sufficeth me: there is no god but He: On Him is my trust,- He the Lord of the Throne (of Glory) Supreme!"

(Verse 10.002) Is it a matter of wonderment to men that We have sent Our inspiration to a man from among themselves?- that he should warn mankind (of their danger), and give the good news to the Believers that they have before their Lord the lofty rank of truth. (But) say the Unbelievers: "This is indeed an evident sorcerer!"

(Verse 12.109) Nor did We send before thee (as messengers) any but men, whom we did inspire,- (men) living in human habitations. Do they not travel through the earth, and see what was the end of those before them? But the home of the hereafter is best, for those who do right. Will ye not then understand?

(Verse 13.030) Thus have we sent thee amongst a People before whom (long since) have (other) Peoples (gone and) passed away; in order that thou mightest rehearse unto them what We send down unto thee by inspiration; yet do they reject (Him), the Most Gracious! Say: "He is my Lord! There is no god but He! On Him is my trust, and to Him do I turn!"

(Verse 13.040) Whether We shall show thee (within thy life-time) part of what we promised them or take to ourselves thy soul (before it is all accomplished),- thy duty is to make (the Message) reach them: it is our part to call them to account.

(Verse 13.043) The Unbelievers say: "No messenger art thou." Say: "Enough for a witness between me and you is Allah, and such as have knowledge of the Book."

(Verse 16.043) And before thee also the messengers We sent were but men, to whom We granted inspiration: if ye realize this not, ask of those who possess the Message. (Verse 16.044) (We sent them) with Clear Signs and Books of dark prophecies; and We have sent down unto thee (also) the Message; that thou mayest explain clearly to men what is sent for them, and that they may give thought.

(Verse 16.082) But if they turn away, thy duty is only to preach the clear Message.

(Verse 17.085) They ask thee concerning the Spirit (of inspiration). Say: "The Spirit (cometh) by command of my Lord: of knowledge it is only a little that is communicated to you, (O men!)" (Verse 17.086) If it were Our Will, We could take away that which We have sent thee by inspiration: then wouldst thou find none to plead thy affair in that matter as against Us,- (Verse 17.087) Except for Mercy from thy Lord: for his bounty is to thee (indeed) great.

(Verse 17.094) What kept men back from belief when Guidance came to them, was nothing but this: they said, "Has Allah sent a man (like us) to be (His) Messenger?" (Verse 17.095) Say, "If there were settled, on earth, angels walking about in peace and quiet, We should certainly have sent them down from the heavens an angel for a messenger." (Verse 17.096) Say: "Enough is Allah for a witness between me and you: for He is well acquainted with His servants, and He sees (all things).

(Verse 18.110) Say: "I am but a man like yourselves, (but) the inspiration has come to me, that your Allah is one Allah: whoever expects to meet his Lord, let him work righteousness, and, in the worship of his Lord, admit no one as partner.

(Verse 21.007) Before thee, also, the messengers We sent were but men, to whom We granted inspiration: If ye realize this not, ask of those who possess the Message. (Verse 21.008) Nor did We give them bodies that ate no food, nor were they exempt from death.

(Verse 21.034) We granted not to any man before thee permanent life (here): if then thou shouldst die, would they live permanently? (Verse 21.035) Every soul shall have a taste of death: and We test you by evil and by good by way of trial. to Us must ye return. (Verse 21.036) When the Unbelievers see thee, they treat thee not except with ridicule. "Is this," (they say), "the one who talks of your gods?" and they blaspheme at the mention of (Allah) Most Gracious!

(Verse 21.107) We sent thee not, but as a Mercy for all creatures. (Verse 21.108) Say: "What has come to me by inspiration is that your Allah is One Allah: will ye therefore bow to His Will (in Islam)?" (Verse 21.109) But if they turn back, Say: "I have proclaimed the Message to you all alike and in truth; but I know not whether that which ye are promised is near or far.

(Verse 22.049) Say: "O men! I am (sent) to you only to give a Clear Warning: (Verse 22.050) "Those who believe and work righteousness, for them is forgiveness and a sustenance most generous. (Verse 22.051) "But those who strive against Our Signs, to frustrate them,- they will be Companions of the

Fire."

(Verse 23.069) Or do they not recognize their Messenger, that they deny him? (Verse 23.070) Or do they say, "He is possessed"? Nay, he has brought them the Truth, but most of them hate the Truth.

(Verse 24.052) It is such as obey Allah and His Messenger, and fear Allah and do right, that will win (in the end), (Verse 24.053) They swear their strongest oaths by Allah that, if only thou wouldst command them, they would leave (their homes). Say: "Swear ye not; Obedience is (more) reasonable; verily, Allah is well acquainted with all that ye do."

(Verse 24.054) Say: "Obey Allah, and obey the Messenger: but if ye turn away, he is only responsible for the duty placed on him and ye for that placed on you. If ye obey him, ye shall be on right guidance. The Messenger's duty is only to preach the clear (Message).

(Verse 25.007) And they say: "What sort of a messenger is this, who eats food, and walks through the streets? Why has not an angel been sent down to him to give admonition with him? (Verse 25.008) "Or (Why) has not a treasure been bestowed on him, or why has he (not) a garden for enjoyment?" The wicked say: "Ye follow none other than a man bewitched." (Verse 25.009) See what kinds of comparisons they make for thee! But they have gone astray, and never a way will they be able to find!

(Verse 25.020) And the messengers whom We sent before thee were all (men) who ate food and walked through the streets: We have made some of you as a trial for others: will ye have patience? for Allah is One Who sees (all things). (Verse 25.021) Such as fear not the meeting with Us (for Judgment) say: "Why are not the angels sent down to us, or (why) do we not see our Lord?" Indeed they have an arrogant conceit of themselves, and mighty is the insolence of their impiety!

(Verse 27.091) For me, I have been commanded to serve the Lord of this city, Him Who has sanctified it and to Whom (belong) all things: and I am commanded to be of those who bow in Islam to Allah's Will,- (Verse 27.092) And to rehearse the Qur'an: and if any accept guidance, they do it for the good of their own souls, and if any stray, say: "I am only a Warner". (Verse 27.093) And say: "Praise be to Allah, Who will soon show you His Signs, so that ye shall know them"; and thy Lord is not unmindful of all that ye do.

(Verse 33.021) Ye have indeed in the Messenger of Allah a beautiful pattern (of conduct) for any one whose hope is in Allah and the Final Day, and who engages much in the Praise of Allah.

(Verse 33.040) Muhammad is not the father of any of your men, but (he is) the Messenger of Allah, and the Seal of the Prophets: and Allah has full knowledge of all things.

(Verse 33.045) O Prophet! Truly We have sent thee as a Witness, a Bearer of Glad Tidings, and Warner,- (Verse 33.046) And as one who invites to Allah's (grace) by His leave, and as a lamp spreading light.

(Verse 33.056) Allah and His angels send blessings on the Prophet: O ye that believe! Send ye blessings on him, and salute him with all respect. (Verse 33.057) Those who annoy Allah and His Messenger - Allah has cursed them in this World and in the Hereafter, and has prepared for them a humiliating Punishment.

(Verse 34.028) We have not sent thee but as a universal (Messenger) to men, giving them glad tidings, and warning them (against sin), but most men understand not.

(Verse 35.023) Thou art no other than a Warner. (Verse 35.024) Verily We have sent thee in truth, as a bearer of glad tidings, and as a Warner: and there never was a people, without a Warner having lived among them (in the past). (Verse 35.025) And if they reject thee, so did their predecessors, to whom came their messengers with Clear Signs, Books of dark prophecies, and the Book of Enlightenment.

(Verse 36.003) Thou art indeed one of the messengers, (Verse 36.004) On a Straight Way.

(Verse 37.035) For they, when they were told that there is no god except Allah, would puff themselves up with Pride, (Verse 37.036) And say: "What! shall we give up our gods for the sake of a Poet possessed?" (Verse 37.037) Nay! he has come with the (very) Truth, and he confirms (the Message of) the messengers (before him).

(Verse 38.065) Say: "Truly am I a Warner: no god is there but the one Allah, Supreme and Irresistible,- (Verse 38.066) "The Lord of the heavens and the earth, and all between,- Exalted in Might, able to enforce His Will, forgiving again and again."

(Verse 41.006) Say thou: "I am but a man like you: It is revealed to me by Inspiration, that your Allah is one Allah: so stand true to Him, and ask for His Forgiveness." And woe to those who join gods with Allah,- (Verse 41.007) Those who practice not regular Charity, and who even deny the Hereafter.

(Verse 42.048) If then they run away, We have not sent thee as a guard over them. Thy duty is but to convey (the Message). And truly, when We give man a taste of a Mercy from Ourselves, he doth exult thereat, but when some ill happens to him, on account of the deeds which his hands have sent forth, truly then is man ungrateful!

(Verse 46.009) Say: "I am no bringer of new-fangled doctrine among the messengers, nor do I know what will be done with me or with you. I follow but that which is revealed to me by inspiration; I am but a Warner open and clear." (Verse 46.010) Say: "See ye? If (this teaching) be from Allah, and ye reject it, and a witness from among the Children of Israel testifies to its similarity (with earlier scripture), and has believed while ye are arrogant, (how unjust ye are!) truly, Allah guides not a people unjust."

(Verse 47.002) But those who believe and work deeds of righteousness, and believe in the (Revelation) sent down to Muhammad - for it is the Truth from their Lord,- He will remove from them their ills and improve their condition.

(Verse 48.008) We have truly sent thee as a witness, as a bringer of Glad Tidings, and as a Warner: (Verse 48.009) In order that ye (O men) may believe in Allah and His Messenger, that ye may assist and honor Him, and celebrate His praise morning and evening.

(Verse 48.028) It is He Who has sent His Messenger with Guidance and the Religion of Truth, to proclaim it over all religion: and enough is Allah for a Witness. (Verse 48.029) Muhammad is the messenger of Allah; and those who are with him are strong against Unbelievers, (but) compassionate amongst each other. Thou wilt see them bow and prostrate themselves (in prayer), seeking Grace from Allah and (His) Good Pleasure. On their faces are their marks, (being) the traces of their prostration. This is their similitude in the Taurat; and their similitude in the Gospel is: like a seed which sends forth its blade, then makes it strong; it then becomes thick, and it stands on its own stem, (filling) the sowers with wonder and delight. As a result, it fills the Unbelievers with rage at them. Allah has promised those among them who believe and do righteous deeds forgiveness, and a great Reward.

(Verse 61.006) And remember, Jesus, the son of Mary, said: "O Children of Israel! I am the messenger of Allah (sent) to you, confirming the Law (which came) before me, and giving Glad Tidings of a Messenger to come after me, whose name shall be Ahmad." But when he came to them with Clear Signs, they said, "this is evident sorcery!"

(Verse 61.009) It is He Who has sent His Messenger with Guidance and the Religion of Truth, that he may proclaim it over all religion, even though the Pagans may detest (it).

(Verse 62.002) It is He Who has sent amongst the Unlettered a messenger from among themselves, to rehearse to them His Signs, to sanctify them, and to instruct them in Scripture and Wisdom,- although they had been, before, in manifest error;- (Verse 62.003) As well as (to confer all these benefits upon) others of them, who have not already joined them: And He is exalted in Might, Wise.

(Verse 64.012) So obey Allah, and obey His Messenger: but if ye turn back, the duty of Our Messenger is but to proclaim (the Message) clearly and openly.

(Verse 68.001) Nun. By the Pen and the (Record) which (men) write,- (Verse 68.002) Thou art not, by the Grace of thy Lord, mad or possessed. (Verse 68.003) Nay, verily for thee is a Reward unfailing: (Verse 68.004) And thou (standest) on an exalted standard of character.

(Verse 69.044) And if the messenger were to invent any sayings in Our name, (Verse 69.045) We should certainly seize him by his right hand, (Verse 69.046) And We should certainly then cut off the artery of his heart: (Verse 69.047) Nor could any of you withhold him (from Our wrath).

(Verse 73.015) We have sent to you, (O men!) a messenger, to be a witness concerning you, even as We sent a messenger to Pharaoh.

(Verse 79.045) Thou art but a Warner for such as fear it.

(Verse 81.019) Verily this is the word of a most honorable Messenger, (Verse 81.020) Endued with Power, with rank before the Lord of the Throne, (Verse 81.021) With authority there, (and) faithful to his trust. (Verse 81.022) And (O people!) your companion is not one possessed; (Verse 81.023) And without doubt he saw him in the clear horizon.

(Verse 88.022) Thou art not one to manage (men's) affairs.

II

Individual Responsibility

Expectations from an Individual

(Verse 2.083) And remember We took a covenant from the Children of Israel (to this effect): Worship none but Allah; treat with kindness your parents and kindred, and orphans and those in need; speak fair to the people; be steadfast in prayer; and practice regular charity. Then did ye turn back, except a few among you, and ye backslide (even now). (Verse 2.084) And remember We took your covenant (to this effect): Shed no blood amongst you, nor turn out your own people from your homes: and this ye solemnly ratified, and to this ye can bear witness.

(Verse 6.151) Say: "Come, I will rehearse what Allah hath (really) prohibited you from": Join not anything as equal with Him; be good to your parents; kill not your children on a plea of want;- We provide sustenance for you and for them;- come not nigh to shameful deeds. Whether open or secret; take not life, which Allah hath made sacred, except by way of justice and law: thus doth He command you, that ye may learn wisdom. (Verse 6.152) And come not nigh to the orphan's property, except to improve it, until he attain the age of full strength; give measure and weight with (full) justice;- no burden do We place on any soul, but that which it can bear;- whenever ye speak, speak justly, even if a near relative is concerned; and fulfill the covenant of Allah: thus doth He command you, that ye may remember. (Verse 6.153) Verily, this is My way, leading straight: follow it: follow not (other) paths: they will scatter you about from His (great) path: thus doth He command you. that ye may be righteous.

(Verse 7.033) Say: the things that my Lord hath indeed forbidden are: shameful deeds, whether open or secret; sins and trespasses against truth or reason; assigning of partners to Allah, for which He hath given no authority; and saying things about Allah of which ye have no knowledge.

(Verse 9.071) The Believers, men and women, are protectors one of another: they enjoin what is just, and forbid what is evil: they observe regular prayers, practice regular charity, and obey Allah and His Messenger. On them will Allah pour His mercy: for Allah is Exalted in power, Wise.

(Verse 13.022) Those who patiently persevere, seeking the countenance of their Lord; Establish regular prayers; spend, out of (the gifts) We have bestowed for their sustenance, secretly and openly; and turn off Evil with good: for such there is the final attainment of the (eternal) home,- (Verse 13.023) Gardens of perpetual bliss: they shall enter there, as well as the righteous among their fathers, their spouses, and their offspring: and angels shall enter unto them from every gate (with the salutation): (Verse 13.024) "Peace unto you for that ye persevered in patience! Now how excellent is the final home!"

(Verse 16.090) Allah commands justice, the doing of good, and liberality to kith and kin, and He forbids all shameful deeds, and injustice and rebellion: He instructs you, that ye may receive admonition. (Verse 16.091) Fulfill the Covenant of Allah when ye have entered into it, and break not your oaths after ye have confirmed them; indeed ye have made Allah your surety; for Allah knoweth all that ye do.

(Verse 23.002) Those who humble themselves in their prayers; (Verse 23.003) Who avoid vain talk; (Verse 23.004) Who are active in deeds of charity; (Verse 23.005) Who abstain from sex, (Verse 23.006) Except with those joined to them in the marriage bond, or (the captives) whom their right hands possess,- for (in their case) they are free from blame, (Verse 23.007) But those whose desires exceed those limits are transgressors;- (Verse 23.008) Those who faithfully observe their trusts and their covenants; (Verse 23.009) And who (strictly) guard their prayers;-

(Verse 25.043) Seest thou such a one as taketh for his god his own passion (or impulse)? Couldst thou be a disposer of affairs for him?

(Verse 25.044) Or thinkest thou that most of them listen or understand? They are only like cattle;- nay, they are worse astray in Path.

(Verse 25.068) Those who invoke not, with Allah, any other god, nor slay such life as Allah has made sacred except for just cause, nor commit fornication; - and any that does this (not only) meets punishment.

(Verse 31.017) "O my son! Establish regular prayer, enjoin what is just, and forbid what is wrong: and bear with patient constancy whatever betide thee; for this is firmness (of purpose) in (the conduct of) affairs. (Verse 31.018) "And swell not thy cheek (for pride) at men, nor walk in insolence through the earth; for Allah loveth not any arrogant boaster. (Verse 31.019) "And be moderate in thy pace, and lower thy voice; for the harshest of sounds without doubt is the braying of the ass."

(Verse 33.023) Among the Believers are men who have been true to their covenant with Allah: of them some have completed their vow (to the extreme), and some (still) wait: but they have never changed (their determination) in the least:

(Verse 33.035) For Muslim men and women,- for believing men and women, for devout men and women, for true men and women, for men and women who are patient and constant, for men and women who humble themselves, for men and women who give in Charity, for men and women who fast (and deny themselves), for men and women who guard their chastity, and for men and women who engage much in Allah's praise,- for them has Allah prepared forgiveness and great reward.

(Verse 41.030) In the case of those who say, "Our Lord is Allah", and, further, stand straight and steadfast, the angels descend on them (from time to time): "Fear ye not!" (they suggest), "Nor grieve! but receive the Glad Tidings of the Garden (of Bliss), the which ye were promised!

(Verse 42.037) Those who avoid the greater crimes and shameful deeds, and, when they are angry even then forgive; (Verse 42.038) Those who hearken to their Lord, and establish regular Prayer; who (conduct) their affairs by mutual Consultation; who spend out of what We bestow on them for Sustenance; (Verse 42.039) And those who, when an oppressive wrong is inflicted on them, (are not cowed but) help and defend themselves.

(Verse 49.015) Only those are Believers who have believed in Allah and His Messenger, and have never since doubted, but have striven with their belongings and their persons in the Cause of Allah: Such are the sincere ones.

(Verse 53.032) Those who avoid great sins and shameful deeds, only (falling into) small faults,- verily thy Lord is ample in forgiveness. He knows you well when He brings you out of the earth, And when ye are hidden in your mothers' wombs. Therefore justify not yourselves: He knows best who it is that guards against evil.

(Verse 57.016) Has not the Time arrived for the Believers that their hearts in all humility should engage in the remembrance of Allah and of the Truth which has been revealed (to them), and that they should not become like those to whom was given Revelation aforetime, but long ages passed over them and their hearts grew hard? For many among them are rebellious transgressors.

(Verse 90.012) And what will explain to thee the path that is steep?- (Verse 90.013) (It is:) freeing the bondman; (Verse 90.014) Or the giving of food in a day of privation (Verse 90.015) To the orphan with claims of relationship, (Verse 90.016) Or to the indigent (down) in the dust. (Verse 90.017) Then will he be of those who believe, and enjoin patience, (constancy, and self-restraint), and enjoin deeds of kindness and compassion. (Verse 90.018) Such are the Companions of the Right Hand.

(Verse 91.007) By the Soul, and the proportion and order given to it; (Verse 91.008) And its enlightenment as to its wrong and its right;- (Verse 91.009) Truly he succeeds that purifies it, (Verse 91.010) And he fails that corrupts it!

(Verse 94.005) So, verily, with every difficulty, there is relief: (Verse 94.006) Verily, with every difficulty there is relief. (Verse 94.007) Therefore, when thou art free (from thine immediate task), still labor hard, (Verse 94.008) And to thy Lord turn (all) thy attention.

Prayer

(Verse 2.003) Who believe in the Unseen, are steadfast in prayer, and spend out of what We have provided for them;

(Verse 2.043) And be steadfast in prayer; practice regular charity; and bow down your heads with those who bow down (in worship).

(Verse 2.110) And be steadfast in prayer and regular in charity: And whatever good ye send forth for your souls before you, ye shall find it with Allah: for Allah sees Well all that ye do.

(Verse 2.183) O ye who believe! Fasting is prescribed to you as it was prescribed to those before you, that ye may (learn) self- restraint,- (Verse2.184) (Fasting) for a fixed number of days; but if any of you is ill, or on a journey, the prescribed number (Should be made up) from days later. For those who can do it (With hardship), is a ransom, the feeding of one that is indigent. But he that will give more, of his own free will,- it is better for him. And it is better for you that ye fast, if ye only knew. (Verse 2.185) Ramadhan is the (month) in which was sent down the Qur'an, as a guide to mankind, also clear (Signs) for guidance and judgment (Between right and wrong). So every one of you who is present (at his home) during that month should spend it in fasting, but if any one is ill, or on a journey, the prescribed period (Should be made up) by days later. Allah intends every facility for you; He does not want to put to difficulties. (He wants you) to complete the prescribed period, and to glorify Him in that He has guided you; and perchance ye shall be grateful. (Verse 2.186) When My servants ask thee concerning Me, I am indeed close (to them): I listen to the prayer of every suppliant when he calleth on Me: Let them also, with a will, Listen to

My call, and believe in Me: That they may walk in the right way.

(Verse 2.187) Permitted to you, on the night of the fasts, is the approach to your wives. They are your garments and ye are their garments. Allah knoweth what ye used to do secretly among yourselves; but He turned to you and forgave you; so now associate with them, and seek what Allah Hath ordained for you, and eat and drink, until the white thread of dawn appear to you distinct from its black thread; then complete your fast Till the night appears; but do not associate with your wives while ye are in retreat in the mosques. Those are Limits (set by) Allah: Approach not nigh thereto. Thus doth Allah make clear His Signs to men: that they may learn self-restraint.

(Verse 3.017) Those who show patience, Firmness and self-control; who are true (in word and deed); who worship devoutly; who spend (in the way of Allah); and who pray for forgiveness in the early hours of the morning.

(Verse 3.135) And those who, having done something to be ashamed of, or wronged their own souls, earnestly bring Allah to mind, and ask for forgiveness for their sins,- and who can forgive sins except Allah?- and are never obstinate in persistently knowingly (the wrong) they have done.

(Verse 4.043) O ye who believe! Approach not prayers with a mind befogged, until ye can understand all that ye say,- nor in a state of ceremonial impurity (Except when travelling on the road), until after washing your whole body. If ye are ill, or on a journey, or one of you cometh from offices of nature, or ye have been in contact with women, and ye find no water, then take for yourselves clean sand or earth, and rub therewith your faces and hands. For Allah doth blot out sins and forgive again and again.

(Verse 4.101) When ye travel through the earth, there is no blame on you if ye shorten your prayers, for fear the Unbelievers May attack you: For the Unbelievers are unto you open enemies.

(Verse 4.102) When thou (O Messenger) art with them, and standest to lead them in prayer, Let one party of them stand up (in prayer) with thee, Taking their arms with them: When they finish their prostrations, let them Take their position in the rear. And let the other party come up which hath not yet prayed - and let them pray with thee, Taking all precaution, and bearing arms: the Unbelievers wish, if ye were negligent of your arms and your baggage, to assault you in a single rush. But there is no blame on you if ye put away your arms because of the inconvenience of rain or because ye are ill; but take (every) precaution for yourselves. For the Unbelievers Allah hath prepared a humiliating punishment. (Verse 4.103) When ye pass (Congregational) prayers, celebrate Allah's praises, standing, sitting down, or lying down on your sides; but when ye are free from danger, set up Regular Prayers: For such prayers are enjoined on believers at stated times.

(Verse 5.006) O ye who believe! when ye prepare for prayer, wash your faces, and your hands (and arms) to the elbows; Rub your heads (with water); and (wash) your feet to the ankles. If ye are in a state of ceremonial impurity, bathe your whole body. But if ye are ill, or on a journey, or one of you cometh from offices of nature, or ye have been in contact with women, and ye find no water, then take for yourselves clean sand or earth, and rub therewith your faces and hands, Allah doth not wish to place you in a difficulty, but to make you clean, and to complete his favour to you, that ye may be grateful.

(Verse 9.018) The mosques of Allah shall be visited and maintained by such as believe in Allah and the Last Day, establish regular prayers, and practice regular charity, and fear none (at all) except Allah. It is they who are expected to be on true guidance.

(Verse 9.112) Those that turn (to Allah) in repentance; that serve Him, and praise Him; that wander in devotion to the cause of Allah,: that bow down and prostrate themselves in prayer; that enjoin good and forbid evil; and observe the limit set by Allah;- (These do rejoice). So proclaim the glad tidings to the Believers.

(Verse 11.114) And establish regular prayers at the two ends of the day and at the approaches of the night: For those things, that are good remove those that are evil: Be that the word of remembrance to those who remember (their Lord): (Verse 11.115) And be steadfast in patience; for verily Allah will not suffer the reward of the righteous to perish.

(Verse 13.014) For Him (alone) is prayer in Truth: any others that they call upon besides Him hear them no more than if they were to stretch forth their hands for water to reach their mouths but it reaches them not: for the prayer of those without Faith is nothing but (futile) wandering (in the mind).

(Verse 14.031) Speak to my servants who have believed, that they may establish regular prayers, and spend (in charity) out of the sustenance we have given them, secretly and openly, before the coming of a Day in which there will be neither mutual bargaining nor befriending.

(Verse 17.078) Establish regular prayers – at the sun's decline till the darkness of the night, and the morning prayer and reading: for the prayer and reading in the morning carry their testimony. (Verse 17.079) And pray in the small watches of the morning: (it would be) an additional prayer (or spiritual profit) for thee: soon will thy Lord raise thee to a Station of Praise and Glory! (Verse 17.080) Say: "O my Lord! Let my entry be by the Gate of Truth and Honor, and likewise my exit by the Gate of Truth and Honor; and grant me from Thy Presence an authority to aid (me)."

(Verse 17.110) Say: "Call upon Allah, or call upon Rahman: by whatever name ye call upon Him, (it is well): for to Him belong the Most Beautiful Names. Neither speak thy Prayer aloud, nor speak it in a low tone, but seek a middle course between."

(Verse 18.055) And what is there to keep back men from believing, now that Guidance has come to them, nor from praying for forgiveness from their Lord, but that (they ask that) the ways of the ancients be repeated with them, or the Wrath be brought to them face to face?

(Verse 20.014) "Verily, I am Allah: There is no god but I: So serve thou Me (only), and establish regular prayer for celebrating My praise.

(Verse 20.130) Therefore be patient with what they say, and celebrate (constantly) the praises of thy Lord, before the rising of the sun, and before its setting; yea, celebrate them for part of the hours of the night, and at the sides of the day: that thou mayest have (spiritual) joy.

(Verse 22.027) "And proclaim the Pilgrimage among men: they will come to thee on foot and (mounted) on every kind of camel, lean on account of journeys through deep and distant mountain highways; (Verse 22.028) "That they may witness the benefits (provided) for them, and celebrate the name of Allah, through the Days appointed, over the cattle which He has provided for them (for sacrifice): then eat ye thereof and feed the distressed ones in want. (Verse 22.029) "Then let them complete the rites prescribed for them, perform their vows, and (again) circumambulate the Ancient House." (Verse 22.030) Such (is the Pilgrimage): whoever honors the sacred rites of Allah, for him it is good in the Sight of his Lord. Lawful to you (for food in Pilgrimage) are cattle, except those mentioned to you (as exception): but shun the abomination of idols, and shun the word that is false,- (Verse 22.31) Being true in faith to Allah, and never assigning partners to Him: if anyone assigns partners to Allah, is as if he had fallen from heaven and been snatched up by birds, or the wind had swooped (like a bird on its prey) and thrown him into a far-distant place.

(Verse 22.035) To those whose hearts when Allah is mentioned, are filled with fear, who show patient perseverance over their afflictions, keep up regular prayer, and spend (in charity) out of what We have bestowed upon them.

(Verse 22.041) (They are) those who, if We establish them in the land, establish regular prayer and give regular charity, enjoin the right and forbid wrong: with Allah rests the end (and decision) of (all) affairs.

(Verse 22.078) And strive in His cause as ye ought to strive, (with sincerity and under discipline). He has chosen you, and has imposed no difficulties on you in religion; it is the cult of your father Abraham. It is He Who has named you Muslims, both before and in this (Revelation); that the Messenger may be a witness for you, and ye be witnesses for mankind! So establish regular Prayer, give regular Charity, and hold fast to Allah! He is your Protector - the Best to protect and the Best to help!

(Verse 24.037) By men whom neither traffic nor merchandise can divert from the Remembrance of Allah, nor from regular Prayer, nor from the practice of regular Charity: Their (only) fear is for the Day when hearts and eyes will be transformed (in a world wholly new),-

(Verse 24.056) So establish regular Prayer and give regular Charity; and obey the Messenger; that ye may receive mercy.

(Verse 25.064)Those who spend the night in adoration of their Lord prostrate and standing; (Verse 25.065) Those who say, "Our Lord! avert from us the Wrath of Hell, for its Wrath is indeed an affliction grievous,- (Verse 25.066) "Evil indeed is it as an abode, and as a place to rest in";

(Verse 27.003) Those who establish regular prayers and give in regular charity, and also have (full) assurance of the hereafter.

(Verse 29.045) Recite what is sent of the Book by inspiration to thee, and establish regular Prayer: for Prayer restrains from shameful and unjust deeds; and remembrance of Allah is the greatest (thing in life) without doubt. And Allah knows the (deeds) that ye do.

(Verse 31.004) Those who establish regular Prayer, and give regular Charity, and have (in their hearts) the assurance of the Hereafter.

(Verse 32.016) Their limbs do forsake their beds of sleep, the while they call on their Lord, in Fear and Hope: and they spend (in charity) out of the sustenance which We have bestowed on them.

(Verse 34.046) Say: "I do admonish you on one point: that ye do stand up before Allah,- (It may be) in pairs, or (it may be) singly,- and reflect (within yourselves): your Companion is not possessed: he is no less than a Warner to you, in face of a terrible Penalty."

(Verse 35.029) Those who rehearse the Book of Allah, establish regular Prayer, and spend (in Charity) out of what We have provided for them, secretly and openly, hope for a commerce that will never fail:

(Verse 39.009) Is one who worships devoutly during the hour of the night prostrating himself or standing (in adoration), who takes heed of the Hereafter, and who places his hope in the Mercy of his Lord - (like one who does not)? Say: "Are those equal, those who know and those who do not know? It is those who are endued with understanding that receive admonition.

(Verse 40.050) They will say: "Did there not come to you your messengers with Clear Signs?" They will say, "Yes". They will reply, "Then pray (as ye like)! But the prayer of those without Faith is nothing but (futile wandering) in (mazes of) error!"

(Verse 50.039) Bear, then, with patience, all that they say, and celebrate the praises of thy Lord, before the rising of the sun and before (its) setting. (Verse 50.040) And during part of the night, (also,) celebrate His praises, and (so likewise) after the postures of adoration.

(Verse 51.017) They were in the habit of sleeping but little by night,

(Verse 51.018) And in the hour of early dawn, they (were found) praying for Forgiveness;

(Verse 62.009) O ye who believe! When the call is proclaimed to prayer on Friday (the Day of Assembly), hasten earnestly to the Remembrance of Allah, and leave off business (and traffic): That is best for you if ye but knew!

(Verse 62.010) And when the Prayer is finished, then may ye disperse through the land, and seek of the Bounty of Allah: and celebrate the Praises of Allah often (and without stint): that ye may prosper.

(Verse 70.034) And those who guard (sacredness) of their worship;- (Verse 70.035) Such will be the honored ones in the Gardens (of Bliss).

(Verse 73.002) Stand (to prayer) by night, but not all night,- (Verse 73.003) Half of it,- or a little less, (Verse 73.004) Or a little more; and recite the Qur'an in slow, measured rhythmic tones.

(Verse 73.006) Truly the rising by night is most potent for governing (the soul), and most suitable for (framing) the Word (of Prayer and Praise).

(Verse 73.020) Thy Lord doth know that thou standest forth (to prayer) nigh two-thirds of the night, or half the night, or a third of the night, and so doth a party of those with thee. But Allah doth appoint night and day in due measure He knoweth that ye are unable to keep count thereof. So He hath turned to you (in mercy): read ye, therefore, of the Qur'an as much as may be easy for you. He knoweth that there may be (some) among you in ill-health; others travelling through the land, seeking of Allah's bounty; yet others fighting in Allah's Cause, read ye, therefore, as much of the Qur'an as may be easy (for you); and establish regular Prayer and give regular Charity; and loan to Allah a Beautiful Loan. And whatever good ye send forth for your souls ye shall find it in Allah's Presence,- yea, better and greater, in Reward and seek ye the Grace of Allah: for Allah is Oft-Forgiving, Most Merciful.

(Verse 76.025) And celebrate the name of thy Lord morning and evening, (Verse 76.026) And part of the night, prostrate thyself to Him; and glorify Him a long night through.

(Verse 107.004) So woe to the worshippers (Verse 107.005) Who are neglectful of their prayers,

Speaking Truth

(Verse 2.042) And cover not Truth with falsehood, nor conceal the
Truth when ye know (what it is).

(Verse 6.115) The word of thy Lord doth find its fulfillment in truth and
in justice: None can change His words: for He is the one who heareth and
knoweth all.

(Verse 9.119) O ye who believe! Fear Allah and be with those who are true
(in word and deed).

(Verse 16.116) But say not - for any false thing that your tongues may put
forth,- "This is lawful, and this is forbidden," so as to ascribe false things to
Allah. For those who ascribe false things to Allah, will never prosper.

(Verse 24.015) Behold, ye received it on your tongues, and said out of your
mouths things of which ye had no knowledge; and ye thought it to be a light
matter, while it was most serious in the sight of Allah. (Verse 24.016) And
why did ye not, when ye heard it, say? - "It is not right of us to speak of this:
Glory to Allah! this is a most serious slander!"

(Verse 25.072) Those who witness no falsehood, and, if they pass by futility,
they pass by it with honorable (avoidance);

(Verse 103.003) Except such as have Faith, and do righteous deeds, and (join
together) in the mutual teaching of Truth, and of Patience and Constancy.

Etiquette

(Verse 4.086) When a (courteous) greeting is offered you, meet it with a greeting still more courteous, or (at least) of equal courtesy. Allah takes careful account of all things.

(Verse 7.146) Those who behave arrogantly on the earth in defiance of right - them will I turn away from My signs: Even if they see all the signs, they will not believe in them; and if they see the way of right conduct, they will not adopt it as the way; but if they see the way of error, that is the way they will adopt. For they have rejected our signs, and failed to take warning from them.

(Verse 17.037) Nor walk on the earth with insolence: for thou canst not rend the earth asunder, nor reach the mountains in height.

(Verse 17.053) Say to My servants that they should (only) say those things that are best: for Satan doth sow dissensions among them: For Satan is to man an avowed enemy.

(Verse 18.023) Nor say of anything, "I shall be sure to do so and so tomorrow"- (Verse 18.024) Without adding, "So please Allah!" and call thy Lord to mind when thou forgettest, and say, "I hope that my Lord will guide me ever closer (even) than this to the right road."

(Verse 24.027) O ye who believe! enter not houses other than your own, until ye have asked permission and saluted those in them: that is best for you, in order that ye may heed (what is seemly). (Verse 24.028) If ye find no one in the house, enter not until permission is given to you: if ye are asked to go back, go back: that makes for greater purity for yourselves: and Allah knows well all that ye do.

(Verse 24.030) Say to the believing men that they should lower their gaze and guard their modesty: that will make for greater purity for them: And Allah is well acquainted with all that they do.

(Verse 24.031) And say to the believing women that they should lower their gaze and guard their modesty; that they should not display their beauty and ornaments except what (must ordinarily) appear thereof; that they should draw their veils over their bosoms and not display their beauty except to their husbands, their fathers, their husband's fathers, their sons, their husbands' sons, their brothers or their brothers' sons, or their sisters' sons, or their women, or the slaves whom their right hands possess, or male servants free of physical needs, or small children who have no sense of the shame of sex; and that they should not strike their feet in order to draw attention to their hidden ornaments. And O ye Believers! turn ye all together towards Allah, that ye may attain Bliss.

(Verse 24.060) Such elderly women as are past the prospect of marriage,- there is no blame on them if they lay aside their (outer) garments, provided they make not a wanton display of their beauty: but it is best for them to be modest: and Allah is One Who sees and knows all things. (Verse 24.061) It is no fault in the blind nor in one born lame, nor in one afflicted with illness, nor in yourselves, that ye should eat in your own houses, or those of your fathers, or your mothers, or your brothers, or your sisters, or your father's brothers or your father's sisters, or your mother's brothers, or your mother's sisters, or in houses of which the keys are in your possession, or in the house of a sincere friend of yours: there is no blame on you, whether ye eat in company or separately. But if ye enter houses, salute each other - a greeting of blessing and purity as from Allah. Thus does Allah make clear the signs to you: that ye may understand. (Verse 24.062) Only those are believers, who believe in Allah and His Messenger: when they are with him on a matter requiring collective action, they do not depart until they have asked for his leave; those who ask for thy leave are those who believe in Allah and His Messenger; so when they ask for thy leave, for some business of theirs, give leave to those of them whom thou wilt, and ask Allah for their forgiveness: for Allah is Oft-Forgiving, Most Merciful.

(Verse 24.063) Deem not the summons of the Messenger among yourselves like the summons of one of you to another: Allah doth know those of you who slip away under shelter of some excuse: then let those beware who withstand the Messenger's order, lest some trial befall them, or a grievous penalty be inflicted on them.

(Verse 25.063) And the servants of (Allah) Most Gracious are those who walk on the earth in humility, and when the ignorant address them, they say, "Peace!";

(Verse 33.058) And those who annoy believing men and women undeservedly, bear (on themselves) a calumny and a glaring sin. (Verse 33.059) O Prophet! Tell thy wives and daughters, and the believing women, that they should cast their outer garments over their persons (when abroad): that is most convenient, that they should be known (as such) and not molested. And Allah is Oft- Forgiving, Most Merciful.

(Verse 49.011) O ye who believe! Let not some men among you laugh at others: It may be that the (latter) are better than the (former): Nor let some women laugh at others: It may be that the (latter are better than the (former): Nor defame nor be sarcastic to each other, nor call each other by (offensive) nicknames: Ill- seeming is a name connoting wickedness, (to be used of one) after he has believed: And those who do not desist are (indeed) doing wrong. (Verse 49.012) O ye who believe! Avoid suspicion as much (as possible): for suspicion in some cases is a sin: And spy not on each other behind their backs. Would any of you like to eat the flesh of his dead brother? Nay, ye would abhor it…But fear Allah: For Allah is Oft-Returning, Most Merciful.

Halal (Kosher)

(Verse 2.168) O ye people! Eat of what is on earth, Lawful and good; and do not follow the footsteps of the evil one, for he is to you an avowed enemy.

(Verse 2.172) O ye who believe! Eat of the good things that We have provided for you, and be grateful to Allah, if it is Him ye worship. (Verse 2.173) He hath only forbidden you dead meat, and blood, and the flesh of swine, and that on which any other name hath been invoked besides that of Allah. But if one is forced by necessity, without willful disobedience, nor transgressing due limits,- then is he guiltless. For Allah is Oft-forgiving Most Merciful.

(Verse 5.001) O ye who believe! fulfill (all) obligations. Lawful unto you (for food) are all four-footed animals, with the exceptions named: But animals of the chase are forbidden while ye are in the sacred precincts or in pilgrim garb: for Allah doth command according to His will and plan. (Verse 5.002) O ye who believe! Violate not the sanctity of the symbols of Allah, nor of the sacred month, nor of the animals brought for sacrifice, nor the garlands that mark out such animals, nor the people resorting to the sacred house, seeking of the bounty and good pleasure of their Lord. But when ye are clear of the sacred precincts and of pilgrim garb, ye may hunt and let not the hatred of some people in (once) shutting you out of the Sacred Mosque lead you to transgression (and hostility on your part). Help ye one another in righteousness and piety, but help ye not one another in sin and rancor: fear Allah: for Allah is strict in punishment.

(Verse 5.003) Forbidden to you (for food) are: dead meat, blood, the flesh of swine, and that on which hath been invoked the name of other than

Allah; that which hath been killed by strangling, or by a violent blow, or by a headlong fall, or by being gored to death; that which hath been (partly) eaten by a wild animal; unless ye are able to slaughter it (in due form); that which is sacrificed on stone (altars); (forbidden) also is the division (of meat) by raffling with arrows: that is impiety. This day have those who reject faith given up all hope of your religion: yet fear them not but fear Me. This day have I perfected your religion for you, completed My favor upon you, and have chosen for you Islam as your religion. But if any is forced by hunger, with no inclination to transgression, Allah is indeed Oft-forgiving, Most Merciful.

(Verse 5.004) They ask thee what is lawful to them (as food). Say: lawful unto you are (all) things good and pure: and what ye have taught your trained hunting animals (to catch) in the manner directed to you by Allah: eat what they catch for you, but pronounce the name of Allah over it: and fear Allah; for Allah is swift in taking account. (Verse 5.005) This day are (all) things good and pure made lawful unto you. The food of the People of the Book is lawful unto you and yours is lawful unto them. (Lawful unto you in marriage) are (not only) chaste women who are believers, but chaste women among the People of the Book, revealed before your time,- when ye give them their due dowers, and desire chastity, not lewdness, nor secret intrigues if any one rejects faith, fruitless is his work, and in the Hereafter he will be in the ranks of those who have lost (all spiritual good).

(Verse 5.087) O ye who believe! make not unlawful the good things which Allah hath made lawful for you, but commit no excess: for Allah loveth not those given to excess.

(Verse 5.090) O ye who believe! Intoxicants and gambling, (dedication of) stones, and (divination by) arrows, are an abomination,- of Satan's handwork: eschew such (abomination), that ye may prosper. (Verse 5.091) Satan's plan is (but) to excite enmity and hatred between you, with intoxicants and gambling, and hinder you from the remembrance of Allah, and from prayer: will ye not then abstain?

(Verse 5.093) On those who believe and do deeds of righteousness there is no blame for what they ate (in the past), when they guard themselves from evil, and believe, and do deeds of righteousness,- (or) again, guard themselves from evil and believe,- (or) again, guard themselves from evil and do good. For Allah loveth those who do good.

(Verse 5.096) Lawful to you is the pursuit of water-game and its use for food,- for the benefit of yourselves and those who travel; but forbidden is the pursuit of land-game;- as long as ye are in the sacred precincts or in pilgrim garb. And fear Allah, to Whom ye shall be gathered back.

(Verse 6.118) So eat of (meats) on which Allah's name hath been pronounced, if ye have faith in His signs. (Verse 6.119) Why should ye not eat of (meats) on which Allah's name hath been pronounced, when He hath explained to you in detail what is forbidden to you - except under compulsion of necessity? But many do mislead (men) by their appetites unchecked by knowledge. Thy Lord knoweth best those who transgress.

(Verse 6.121) Eat not of (meats) on which Allah's name hath not been pronounced: That would be impiety. But the evil ones ever inspire their friends to contend with you if ye were to obey them, ye would indeed be Pagans.

(Verse 6.138) And they say that such and such cattle and crops are taboo, and none should eat of them except those whom - so they say - We wish; further, there are cattle forbidden to yoke or burden, and cattle on which, (at slaughter), the name of Allah is not pronounced; - inventions against Allah's name: soon will He requite them for their inventions. (Verse 6.139) They say: "What is in the wombs of such and such cattle is especially reserved (for food) for our men, and forbidden to our women; but if it is still- born, then all have share therein. For their (false) attribution (of superstitions to Allah), He will soon punish them: for He is full of wisdom and knowledge.

(Verse 6.140) Lost are those who slay their children, from folly, without knowledge, and forbid food which Allah hath provided for them, inventing (lies) against Allah. They have indeed gone astray and heeded no guidance.

(Verse 6.141) It is He Who produceth gardens, with trellises and without, and dates, and tilth with produce of all kinds, and olives and pomegranates, similar (in kind) and different (in variety): eat of their fruit in their season, but render the dues that are proper on the day that the harvest is gathered.

But waste not by excess: for Allah loveth not the wasters.

(Verse 6.142) Of the cattle are some for burden and some for meat: eat what Allah hath provided for you, and follow not the footsteps of Satan: for he is to you and avowed enemy. (Verse 6.143) (Take) eight (head of cattle) in (four) pairs: of sheep a pair, and of goats a pair; say, hath He forbidden the two males, or the two females, or (the young) which the wombs of the two females enclose? Tell me with knowledge if ye are truthful: (Verse 6.144) Of camels a pair, and oxen a pair; say, hath He forbidden the two males, or the two females, or (the young) which the wombs of the two females enclose? - Were ye present when Allah ordered you such a thing? But who doth more wrong than one who invents a lie against Allah, to lead astray men without knowledge? For Allah guideth not people who do wrong. (Verse 6.145) Say: "I find not in the message received by me by inspiration any (meat) forbidden to be eaten by one who wishes to eat it, unless it be dead meat, or blood poured forth, or the flesh of swine,- for it is an abomination - or, what is impious, (meat) on which a name has been invoked, other than Allah's". But (even so), if a person is forced by necessity, without willful disobedience, nor transgressing due limits,- thy Lord is Oft- forgiving, Most Merciful.

(Verse 6.146) For those who followed the Jewish Law, We forbade every (animal) with undivided hoof, and We forbade them that fat of the ox and the sheep, except what adheres to their backs or their entrails, or is mixed up with a bone: this in recompense for their willful disobedience: for We are true (in Our ordinances).

(Verse 10.059) Say: "See ye what things Allah hath sent down to you for sustenance? Yet ye hold forbidden some things thereof and (some things) lawful." Say: "Hath Allah indeed permitted you, or do ye invent (things) to attribute to Allah?"

(Verse 16.005) And cattle He has created for you (men): from them ye derive warmth, and numerous benefits, and of their (meat) ye eat.

(Verse 16.068) And thy Lord taught the Bee to build its cells in hills, on trees, and in (men's) habitations; (verse 16.069) Then to eat of all the produce (of the earth), and find with skill the spacious paths of its Lord: there issues from within their bodies a drink of varying colors, wherein is healing for men: verily in this is a Sign for those who give thought.

(Verse 16.114) So eat of the sustenance which Allah has provided for you, lawful and good: and be grateful for the favors of Allah, if it is He whom ye serve. (Verse 16.115) He has only forbidden you dead meat, and blood, and the flesh of swine, and any (food) over which the name of other than Allah has been invoked. But if one is forced by necessity, without willful disobedience, nor transgressing due limits,- then Allah is oft-forgiving, Most Merciful.

(Verse 66.001) O Prophet! Why holdest thou to be forbidden that which Allah has made lawful to thee? Thou seekest to please thy consorts. But Allah is Oft-Forgiving, Most Merciful.

Rejecting Faith & Hypocrisy

(Verse 3.086) How shall Allah Guide those who reject Faith after they accepted it and bore witness that the Messenger was true and that Clear Signs had come unto them? but Allah guides not a people unjust.

(Verse 3.090) But those who reject Faith after they accepted it, and then go on adding to their defiance of Faith,- never will their repentance be accepted; for they are those who have (of set purpose) gone astray.

(Verse 9.064) The Hypocrites are afraid lest a Sura should be sent down about them, showing them what is (really passing) in their hearts. Say: "Mock ye! But verily Allah will bring to light all that ye fear (should be revealed). (Verse 9.065) If thou dost question them, they declare (with emphasis): "We were only talking idly and in play." Say: "Was it at Allah, and His Signs, and His Messenger, that ye were mocking?" (Verse 9.066) Make ye no excuses: ye have rejected Faith after ye had accepted it. If We pardon some of you, We will punish others amongst you, for that they are in sin. (Verse 9.067) The Hypocrites, men and women, (have an understanding) with each other: They enjoin evil, and forbid what is just, and are close with their hands. They have forgotten Allah; so He hath forgotten them. Verily the Hypocrites are rebellious and perverse. (Verse 9.068) Allah hath promised the Hypocrites men and women, and the rejecters, of Faith, the fire of Hell: Therein shall they dwell: Sufficient is it for them: for them is the curse of Allah, and an enduring punishment,-

(Verse 16.091) Fulfill the Covenant of Allah when ye have entered into it, and break not your oaths after ye have confirmed them; indeed ye have made Allah your surety; for Allah knoweth all that ye do.

(Verse 16.106) Any one who, after accepting faith in Allah, utters Unbelief,- except under compulsion, his heart remaining firm in Faith - but such as open their breast to Unbelief, on them is Wrath from Allah, and theirs will be a dreadful Penalty.

(Verse 29.010) Then there are among men such as say, "We believe in Allah"; but when they suffer affliction in (the cause of) Allah, they treat men's oppression as if it were the Wrath of Allah! And if help comes (to thee) from thy Lord, they are sure to say, "We have (always) been with you!" Does not Allah know best all that is in the hearts of all creation? (Verse 29.011) And Allah most certainly knows those who believe, and as certainly those who are Hypocrites.

(Verse 33.013) Behold! A party among them said: "Ye men of Yathrib! ye cannot stand (the attack)! therefore go back!" And a band of them ask for leave of the Prophet, saying, "Truly our houses are bare and exposed," though they were not exposed they intended nothing but to run away.

(Verse 33.72) We did indeed offer the Trust to the Heavens and the Earth and the Mountains; but they refused to undertake it, being afraid thereof: but man undertook it;- He was indeed unjust and foolish;- (Verse 33.73) (With the result) that Allah has to punish the Hypocrites, men and women, and the Unbelievers, men and women, and Allah turns in Mercy to the Believers, men and women: for Allah is Oft-Forgiving, Most Merciful.

(Verse 42.016) But those who dispute concerning Allah after He has been accepted,- futile is their dispute in the Sight of their Lord: on them will be a Penalty terrible.

(Verse 43.087) If thou ask them, who created them, they will certainly say, Allah: How then are they deluded away (from the Truth)?

(Verse 47.025) Those who turn back as apostates after Guidance was clearly shown to them,- the Evil One has instigated them and busied them up with false hopes. (Verse 47.026) This, because they said to those who hate what Allah has revealed, "We will obey you in part of (this) matter"; but Allah knows their (inner) secrets.

(Verse 47.030) Had We so wiled, We could have shown them up to thee, and thou shouldst have known them by their marks: but surely thou wilt know them by the tone of their speech! And Allah knows all that ye do.

(Verse 48.006) And that He may punish the Hypocrites, men and women, and the Polytheists men and women, who imagine an evil opinion of Allah. On them is a round of Evil: the Wrath of Allah is on them: He has cursed them and got Hell ready for them: and evil is it for a destination.

(Verse 49.017) They impress on thee as a favor that they have embraced Islam. Say, "Count not your Islam as a favor upon me: Nay, Allah has conferred a favor upon you that He has guided you to the faith, if ye be true and sincere.

(Verse 57.013) One Day will the Hypocrites- men and women - say to the Believers: "Wait for us! Let us borrow (a Light) from your Light!" It will be said: "Turn ye back to your rear! then seek a Light (where ye can)!" So a wall will be put up betwixt them, with a gate therein. Within it will be Mercy throughout, and without it, all alongside, will be (Wrath and) Punishment! (Verse 57.014) (Those without) will call out, "Were we not with you?" (The others) will reply, "True! but ye led yourselves into temptation; ye looked forward (to our ruin); ye doubted (Allah's Promise); and (your false) desires deceived you; until there issued the Command of Allah. And the Deceiver deceived you in respect of Allah.

(Verse 63.001) When the Hypocrites come to thee, they say, "We bear witness that thou art indeed the Messenger of Allah." Yea, Allah knoweth that thou art indeed His Messenger, and Allah beareth witness that the Hypocrites are indeed liars.

(Verse 63.002) They have made their oaths a screen (for their misdeeds): thus they obstruct (men) from the Path of Allah: truly evil are their deeds. (Verse 63.003) That is because they believed, then they rejected Faith: So a seal was set on their hearts: therefore they understand not.

(Verse 63.004) When thou lookest at them, their exteriors please thee; and when they speak, thou listenest to their words. They are as (worthless as hollow) pieces of timber propped up, (unable to stand on their own). They think that every cry is against them. They are the enemies; so beware of them. The curse of Allah be on them! How are they deluded (away from the Truth)! (Verse 63.005) And when it is said to them, "Come, the Messenger of

Allah will pray for your forgiveness", they turn aside their heads, and thou wouldst see them turning away their faces in arrogance.

54

Abstinence & Perseverance

(Verse 3.017) Those who show patience, firmness and self-control; who are true (in word and deed); who worship devoutly; who spend (in the way of Allah); and who pray for forgiveness in the early hours of the morning.

(Verse 3.134) Those who spend (freely), whether in prosperity, or in adversity; who restrain anger, and pardon (all) men;- for Allah loves those who do good;- (Verse 3.135) And those who, having done something to be ashamed of, or wronged their own souls, earnestly bring Allah to mind, and ask for forgiveness for their sins,- and who can forgive sins except Allah?- and are never obstinate in persisting knowingly in (the wrong) they have done.

(Verse 3.200) O ye who believe! Persevere in patience and constancy; vie in such perseverance; strengthen each other; and fear Allah; that ye may prosper.

(Verse 4.135) O ye who believe! Stand out firmly for justice, as witnesses to Allah, even as against yourselves, or your parents, or your kin, and whether it be (against) rich or poor: for Allah can best protect both. Follow not the lusts (of your hearts), lest ye swerve, and if ye distort (justice) or decline to do justice, verily Allah is well-acquainted with all that ye do.

(Verse 7.032) Say: Who hath forbidden the beautiful (gifts) of Allah, which He hath produced for His servants, and the things, clean and pure, (which He hath provided) for sustenance? Say: They are, in the life of this world, for those who believe, (and) purely for them on the Day of Judgment. Thus do We explain the signs in detail for those who understand. (Verse 7.033) Say: the things that my Lord hath indeed forbidden are: shameful deeds, whether open or secret; sins and trespasses against truth or reason; assigning of partners to Allah, for which He hath given no authority; and saying things about Allah of which ye have no knowledge.

(Verse 8.046) And obey Allah and His Messenger; and fall into no disputes, lest ye lose heart and your power depart; and be patient and persevering: For Allah is with those who patiently persevere: (Verse 8.047) And be not like those who started from their homes insolently and to be seen of men, and to hinder (men) from the path of Allah: For Allah compasseth round about all that they do.

(Verse 13.022) Those who patiently persevere, seeking the countenance of their Lord; establish regular prayers; spend, out of (the gifts) We have bestowed for their sustenance, secretly and openly; and turn off Evil with good: for such there is the final attainment of the (eternal) home,- (Verse 13.023) Gardens of perpetual bliss: they shall enter there, as well as the righteous among their fathers, their spouses, and their offspring: and angels shall enter unto them from every gate (with the salutation): (Verse 13.024) "Peace unto you for that ye persevered in patience! Now how excellent is the final home!"

(Verse 22.035) To those whose hearts when Allah is mentioned, are filled with fear, who show patient perseverance over their afflictions, keep up regular prayer, and spend (in charity) out of what We have bestowed upon them.

(Verse 28.050) But if they hearken not to thee, know that they only follow their own lusts: and who is more astray than one who follow his own lusts, devoid of guidance from Allah? for Allah guides not people given to wrong-doing.

(Verse 28.053) And when it is recited to them, they say: "We believe therein, for it is the Truth from our Lord: indeed we have been Muslims (bowing to Allah's Will) from before this. (Verse 28.054) Twice will they be given their reward, for that they have persevered, that they avert Evil with Good, and that they spend (in charity) out of what We have given them.

(Verse 33.035) For Muslim men and women,- for believing men and women, for devout men and women, for true men and women, for men and women who are patient and constant, for men and women who humble themselves, for men and women who give in Charity, for men and women who fast (and deny themselves), for men and women who guard their chastity, and for men and women who engage much in Allah's praise,- for them has Allah prepared forgiveness and great reward.

(Verse 45.023) Then seest thou such a one as takes as his god his own vain desire? Allah has, knowing (him as such), left him astray, and sealed his hearing and his heart (and understanding), and put a cover on his sight. Who, then, will guide him after Allah (has withdrawn Guidance)? Will ye not then receive admonition?

(Verse 54.003) They reject (the warning) and follow their (own) lusts but every matter has its appointed time.

(Verse 103.003) Except such as have Faith, and do righteous deeds, and (join together) in the mutual teaching of Truth, and of Patience and Constancy.

III

Family Matters

Institution of Marriage

(Verse 2.221) Do not marry unbelieving women (idolaters), until they believe: A slave woman who believes is better than an unbelieving woman, even though she allures you. Nor marry (your girls) to unbelievers until they believe: A man slave who believes is better than an unbeliever, even though he allures you. Unbelievers do (but) beckon you to the Fire. But Allah beckons by His Grace to the Garden (of bliss) and forgiveness, and makes His Signs clear to mankind: That they may celebrate His praise.

(Verse 4.003) If ye fear that ye shall not be able to deal justly with the orphans, Marry women of your choice, Two or three or four; but if ye fear that ye shall not be able to deal justly (with them), then only one, or (a captive) that your right hands possess, that will be more suitable, to prevent you from doing injustice. (Verse 4.004) And give the women (on marriage) their dower as a free gift; but if they, of their own good pleasure, remit any part of it to you, Take it and enjoy it with right good cheer. (Verse 4.005) To those weak of understanding Make not over your property, which Allah hath made a means of support for you, but feed and clothe them therewith, and speak to them words of kindness and justice.

(Verse 4.019) O ye who believe! Ye are forbidden to inherit women against their will. Nor should ye treat them with harshness, that ye may take away part of the dower ye have given them,-except where they have been guilty of open lewdness; on the contrary live with them on a footing of kindness and equity. If ye take a dislike to them it may be that ye dislike a thing, and Allah brings about through it a great deal of good. (Verse 4.020) But if ye decide to take one wife in place of another, even if ye had given the latter a whole treasure for dower, Take not the least bit of it back: Would ye take it by slander and manifest wrong? (Verse 4.021) And how could ye take it when ye have gone in unto each other, and they have Taken from you a solemn covenant? (Verse 4.022) And marry not women whom your fathers married,- except what is past: It was shameful and odious,- an abominable custom indeed.

(Verse 4.023) Prohibited to you (For marriage) are:- Your mothers, daughters, sisters; father's sisters, Mother's sisters; brother's daughters, sister's daughters; foster-mothers (Who gave you suck), foster-sisters; your wives' mothers; your step-daughters under your guardianship, born of your wives to whom ye have gone in,- no prohibition if ye have not gone in;- (Those who have been) wives of your sons proceeding from your loins; and two sisters in wedlock at one and the same time, except for what is past; for Allah is Oft-forgiving, Most Merciful;- (Verse 4.024) Also (prohibited are) women already married, except those whom your right hands possess: Thus hath Allah ordained (Prohibitions) against you: Except for these, all others are lawful, provided ye seek (them in marriage) with gifts from your property,- desiring chastity, not lust, seeing that ye derive benefit from them, give them their dowers (at least) as prescribed; but if, after a dower is prescribed, agree Mutually (to vary it), there is no blame on you, and Allah is All-knowing, All-wise. (Verse 4.025) If any of you have not the means wherewith to wed free believing women, they may wed believing girls from among those whom your right hands possess: And Allah hath full knowledge about your faith. Ye are one from another: Wed them with the leave of their owners, and give them their dowers, according to what is reasonable: They should be chaste, not lustful, nor taking paramours: when they are taken in wedlock, if they fall into shame, their punishment is half that for free women. This (permission) is for those among you who fear sin; but it is better for you that ye practice self-restraint. And Allah is Oft-forgiving, Most Merciful.

(Verse 5.005) This day are (all) things good and pure made lawful unto you. The food of the People of the Book is lawful unto you and yours is lawful unto them. (Lawful unto you in marriage) are (not only) chaste women who are believers, but chaste women among the People of the Book, revealed before your time,- when ye give them their due dowers, and desire chastity, not lewdness, nor secret intrigues if any one rejects faith, fruitless is his work, and in the Hereafter he will be in the ranks of those who have lost (all spiritual good).

(Verse 24.003) Let no man guilty of adultery or fornication marry and but a woman similarly guilty, or an Unbeliever: nor let any but such a man or an Unbeliever marry such a woman: to the Believers such a thing is forbidden.

(Verse 24.026) Women impure are for men impure, and men impure for women impure and women of purity are for men of purity, and men of purity are for women of purity: these are not affected by what people say: for them there is forgiveness, and a provision honorable.

(Verse 24.032) Marry those among you who are single, or the virtuous ones among yourselves, male or female: if they are in poverty, Allah will give them means out of His grace: for Allah encompasseth all, and he knoweth all things. (Verse 24.033) Let those who find not the wherewithal for marriage keep themselves chaste, until Allah gives them means out of His grace. And if any of your slaves ask for a deed in writing (to enable them to earn their freedom for a certain sum), give them such a deed if ye know any good in them: yea, give them something yourselves out of the means which Allah has given to you. But force not your maids to prostitution when they desire chastity, in order that ye may make a gain in the goods of this life. But if anyone compels them, yet, after such compulsion, is Allah, Oft-Forgiving, Most Merciful (to them),

(Verse 25.054) It is He Who has created man from water: then has He established relationships of lineage and marriage: for thy Lord has power (over all things).

(Verse 33.037) Behold! Thou didst say to one who had received the grace of Allah and thy favor: "Retain thou (in wedlock) thy wife, and fear Allah." But thou didst hide in thy heart that which Allah was about to make manifest: thou didst fear the people, but it is more fitting that thou shouldst fear Allah. Then when Zaid had dissolved (his marriage) with her, with the necessary (formality), We joined her in marriage to thee: in order that (in future) there may be no difficulty to the Believers in (the matter of) marriage with the wives of their adopted sons, when the latter have dissolved with the necessary (formality) (their marriage) with them. And Allah's command must be fulfilled.

(Verse 60.010) O ye who believe! When there come to you believing women refugees, examine (and test) them: Allah knows best as to their Faith: if ye ascertain that they are Believers, then send them not back to the Unbelievers. They are not lawful (wives) for the Unbelievers, nor are the (Unbelievers) lawful (husbands) for them. But pay the Unbelievers what they have spent (on their dower), and there will be no blame on you if ye marry them on payment of their dower to them. But hold not to the guardianship of unbelieving women: ask for what ye have spent on their dowers, and let the (Unbelievers) ask for what they have spent (on the dowers of women who come over to you). Such is the command of Allah: He judges (with justice) between you. And Allah is Full of Knowledge and Wisdom. (Verse 60.011) And if any of your wives deserts you to the Unbelievers, and ye have an accession (by the coming over of a woman from the other side), then pay to those whose wives have deserted the equivalent of what they had spent (on their dower). And fear Allah, in Whom ye believe.

Marital Relations

(Verse 2.187) Permitted to you, on the night of the fasts, is the approach to your wives. They are your garments and ye are their garments. Allah knoweth what ye used to do secretly among yourselves; but He turned to you and forgave you; so now associate with them, and seek what Allah Hath ordained for you, and eat and drink, until the white thread of dawn appear to you distinct from its black thread; then complete your fast Till the night appears; but do not associate with your wives while ye are in retreat in the mosques. Those are Limits (set by) Allah: Approach not nigh thereto. Thus doth Allah make clear His Signs to men: that they may learn self-restraint.

(Verse 2.222) They ask thee concerning women's courses. Say: They are a hurt and a pollution: So keep away from women in their courses, and do not approach them until they are clean. But when they have purified themselves, ye may approach them in any manner, time, or place ordained for you by Allah. For Allah loves those who turn to Him constantly and He loves those who keep themselves pure and clean. (Verse 2.223) Your wives are as a tilth unto you; so approach your tilth when or how ye will; but do some good act for your souls beforehand; and fear Allah. And know that ye are to meet Him (in the Hereafter), and give (these) good tidings to those who believe.

(Verse 4.001) O mankind! reverence your Guardian-Lord, who created you from a single person, created, of like nature, His mate, and from them twain scattered (like seeds) countless men and women;- reverence Allah, through whom ye demand your mutual (rights), and (reverence) the wombs (That bore you): for Allah ever watches over you.

(Verse 4.019) O ye who believe! Ye are forbidden to inherit women against their will. Nor should ye treat them with harshness, that ye may Take away part of the dower ye have given them,-except where they have been guilty of open lewdness; on the contrary live with them on a footing of kindness and equity. If ye take a dislike to them it may be that ye dislike a thing, and Allah brings about through it a great deal of good.

(Verse 4.034) Men are the protectors and maintainers of women, because Allah has given the one more (strength) than the other, and because they support them from their means. Therefore the righteous women are devoutly obedient, and guard in (the husband's) absence what Allah would have them guard.

As to those women on whose part ye fear disloyalty and ill- conduct, admonish them (first), (Next), refuse to share their beds, (And last) beat them (lightly); but if they return to obedience, seek not against them Means (of annoyance): For Allah is Most High, great (above you all). (Verse 4.035) If ye fear a breach between them twain, appoint (two) arbiters, one from his family, and the other from hers; if they wish for peace, Allah will cause their reconciliation: For Allah hath full knowledge, and is acquainted with all things.

(Verse 7.189) It is He Who created you from a single person, and made his mate of like nature, in order that he might dwell with her (in love). When they are united, she bears a light burden and carries it about (unnoticed). When she grows heavy, they both pray to Allah their Lord, (saying): "If Thou givest us a goodly child, we vow we shall (ever) be grateful." (Verse 7.190) But when He giveth them a goodly child, they ascribe to others a share in the gift they have received: but Allah is exalted high above the partners they ascribe to Him.

(Verse 16.072) And Allah has made for you mates (and companions) of your own nature, and made for you, out of them, sons and daughters and grandchildren, and provided for you sustenance of the best: will they then believe in vain things, and be ungrateful for Allah's favors?- (Verse 16.073) And worship others than Allah,- such as have no power of providing them, for sustenance, with anything in heavens or earth, and cannot possibly have such power?

(Verse 24.026) Women impure are for men impure, and men impure for women impure and women of purity are for men of purity, and men of purity are for women of purity: these are not affected by what people say: for them there is forgiveness, and a provision honorable.

(Verse 30.021) And among His Signs is this, that He created for you mates from among yourselves, that ye may dwell in tranquility with them, and He has put love and mercy between your (hearts): verily in that are Signs for those who reflect.

(Verse 52.021) And those who believe and whose families follow them in Faith,- to them shall We join their families: Nor shall We deprive them (of the fruit) of aught of their works: (Yet) is each individual in pledge for his deeds.

(Verse 53.043) That it is He Who granteth Laughter and Tears; (Verse 53.044) That it is He Who granteth Death and Life; (Verse 53.045) That He did create in pairs,- male and female, (Verse 53.046) From a seed when lodged (in its place); (Verse 53.047) That He hath promised a Second Creation (Raising of the Dead); (Verse 53.048) That it is He Who giveth wealth and satisfaction;

(Verse 58.001) Allah has indeed heard (and accepted) the statement of the woman who pleads with thee concerning her husband and carries her complaint (in prayer) to Allah: and Allah (always) hears the arguments between both sides among you: for Allah hears and sees (all things).

(Verse 64.014) O ye who believe! Truly, among your wives and your children are (some that are) enemies to yourselves: so beware of them! But if ye forgive and overlook, and cover up (their faults), verily Allah is Oft-Forgiving, Most Merciful.

(Verse 66.010) Allah sets forth, for an example to the Unbelievers, the wife of Noah and the wife of Lut: they were (respectively) under two of our righteous servants, but they were false to their (husbands), and they profited nothing before Allah on their account, but were told: "Enter ye the Fire along with (others) that enter!" (Verse 66.011) And Allah sets forth, as an example to those who believe the wife of Pharaoh: Behold she said: "O my Lord! Build for me, in nearness to Thee, a mansion in the Garden, and save me from Pharaoh and his doings, and save me from those that do wrong"; (Verse 66.012) And Mary the daughter of 'Imran, who guarded her chastity; and We breathed into (her body) of Our spirit; and she testified to the truth of the words of her Lord and of His Revelations, and was one of the devout (servants).

(Verse 70.029) And those who guard their chastity, (Verse 70.030) Except with their wives and the (captives) whom their right hands possess,- for (then) they are not to be blamed,

(Verse 75.039) And of him He made two sexes, male and female.

Extra Marital Affairs

(Verse 17.032) Nor come nigh to adultery: for it is a shameful (deed) and an evil, opening the road (to other evils).

(Verse 24.002) The woman and the man guilty of adultery or fornication,- flog each of them with a hundred stripes: Let not compassion move you in their case, in a matter prescribed by Allah, if ye believe in Allah and the Last Day: and let a party of the Believers witness their punishment.

(Verse 24.004) And those who launch a charge against chaste women, and produce not four witnesses (to support their allegations),- flog them with eighty stripes; and reject their evidence ever after: for such men are wicked transgressors;- (Verse 24.005) Unless they repent thereafter and mend (their conduct); for Allah is Oft-Forgiving, Most Merciful. (Verse 24.006) And for those who launch a charge against their spouses, and have (in support) no evidence but their own,- their solitary evidence (can be received) if they bear witness four times (with an oath) by Allah that they are solemnly telling the truth; (Verse 24.007) And the fifth (oath) (should be) that they solemnly invoke the curse of Allah on themselves if they tell a lie. (Verse 24.008) But it would avert the punishment from the wife, if she bears witness four times (with an oath) By Allah, that (her husband) is telling a lie; (Verse 24.009) And the fifth (oath) should be that she solemnly invokes the wrath of Allah on herself if (her accuser) is telling the truth.

(Verse 24.012) Why did not the believers - men and women - when ye heard of the affair,- put the best construction on it in their own minds and say, "This (charge) is an obvious lie"? (Verse 24.013) Why did they not bring four witnesses to prove it? When they have not brought the witnesses, such men, in the sight of Allah, (stand forth) themselves as liars! (Verse 24.014) Were it not for the grace and mercy of Allah on you, in this world and the Hereafter, a grievous penalty would have seized you in that ye rushed glibly into this affair.

Verse 24.023) Those who slander chaste women, indiscreet but believing, are cursed in this life and in the Hereafter: for them is a grievous Penalty,- (Verse 24.024) On the Day when their tongues, their hands, and their feet will bear witness against them as to their actions.

Divorce

(Verse 2.226) For those who take an oath for abstention from their wives, a waiting for four months is ordained; if then they return, Allah is Oft-forgiving, Most Merciful. (Verse 2.227) But if their intention is firm for divorce, Allah heareth and knoweth all things.

(Verse 2.228) Divorced women shall wait concerning themselves for three monthly periods. Nor is it lawful for them to hide what Allah Hath created in their wombs, if they have faith in Allah and the Last Day. And their husbands have the better right to take them back in that period, if they wish for reconciliation. And women shall have rights similar to the rights against them, according to what is equitable; but men have a degree (of advantage) over them. And Allah is Exalted in Power, Wise.

(Verse 2.229) A divorce is only permissible twice: after that, the parties should either hold Together on equitable terms, or separate with kindness. It is not lawful for you, (Men), to take back any of your gifts (from your wives), except when both parties fear that they would be unable to keep the limits ordained by Allah. If ye (judges) do indeed fear that they would be unable to keep the limits ordained by Allah, there is no blame on either of them if she give something for her freedom. These are the limits ordained by Allah; so do not transgress them if any do transgress the limits ordained by Allah, such persons wrong (Themselves as well as others).

(Verse 2.230) So if a husband divorces his wife (irrevocably), He cannot, after that, re-marry her until after she has married another husband and He has divorced her. In that case there is no blame on either of them if they re-unite, provided they feel that they can keep the limits ordained by Allah.

Such are the limits ordained by Allah, which He makes plain to those who understand.

(Verse 2.231) When ye divorce women, and they fulfill the term of their ('Iddat), either take them back on equitable terms or set them free on equitable terms; but do not take them back to injure them, (or) to take undue advantage; if any one does that; He wrongs his own soul. Do not treat Allah's Signs as a jest, but solemnly rehearse Allah's favors on you, and the fact that He sent down to you the Book and Wisdom, for your instruction. And fear Allah, and know that Allah is well acquainted with all things.

(Verse 2.232) When ye divorce women, and they fulfill the term of their ('Iddat), do not prevent them from marrying their (former) husbands, if they mutually agree on equitable terms. This instruction is for all amongst you, who believe in Allah and the Last Day. That is (the course Making for) most virtue and purity amongst you and Allah knows, and ye know not.

(Verse 2.236) There is no blame on you if ye divorce women before consummation or the fixation of their dower; but bestow on them (A suitable gift), the wealthy according to his means, and the poor according to his means;- A gift of a reasonable amount is due from those who wish to do the right thing. (Verse 2.237) And if ye divorce them before consummation, but after the fixation of a dower for them, then the half of the dower (Is due to them), unless they remit it or (the man's half) is remitted by him in whose hands is the marriage tie; and the remission (of the man's half) is the nearest to righteousness. And do not forget Liberality between yourselves. For Allah sees well all that ye do.

(Verse 2.241) For divorced women maintenance (should be provided) on a reasonable (scale). This is a duty on the righteous.

(Verse 4.035) If ye fear a breach between them twain, appoint (two) arbiters, one from his family, and the other from hers; if they wish for peace, Allah will cause their reconciliation: For Allah hath full knowledge, and is acquainted with all things.

(Verse 4.128) If a wife fears cruelty or desertion on her husband's part, there is no blame on them if they arrange an amicable settlement between themselves; and such settlement is best; even though men's souls are swayed by greed. But if ye do good and practice self-restraint, Allah is well-acquainted with all that ye do. (Verse 4.129) Ye are never able to be fair and just as between women, even if it is your ardent desire: But turn not away (from a woman) altogether, so as to leave her (as it were) hanging (in the air). If ye come to a friendly understanding, and practice self- restraint, Allah is Oft-forgiving, Most Merciful. (Verse 4.130) But if they disagree (and must part), Allah will provide abundance for all from His all-reaching bounty: for Allah is He that careth for all and is Wise.

(Verse 33.049) O ye who believe! When ye marry believing women, and then divorce them before ye have touched them, no period of 'Iddat have ye to count in respect of them: so give them a present. And set them free in a handsome manner.

(Verse 58.003) But those who divorce their wives by Zihar, then wish to go back on the words they uttered,- (It is ordained that such a one) should free a slave before they touch each other: Thus are ye admonished to perform: and Allah is well-acquainted with (all) that ye do. (Verse 58.004) And if any has not (the wherewithal), he should fast for two months consecutively before they touch each other. But if any is unable to do so, he should feed sixty indigent ones, this, that ye may show your faith in Allah and His Messenger. Those are limits (set by) Allah. For those who reject (Him), there is a grievous Penalty.

(Verse 65.001) O Prophet! When ye do divorce women, divorce them at their prescribed periods, and count (accurately), their prescribed periods: And fear Allah your Lord: and turn them not out of their houses, nor shall they (themselves) leave, except in case they are guilty of some open lewdness, those are limits set by Allah: and any who transgresses the limits of Allah, does verily wrong his (own) soul: thou knowest not if perchance Allah will bring about thereafter some new situation.

(Verse 65.002) Thus when they fulfill their term appointed, either take them back on equitable terms or part with them on equitable terms; and take for witness two persons from among you, endued with justice, and establish the evidence (as) before Allah. Such is the admonition given to him who believes in Allah and the Last Day. And for those who fear Allah, He (ever) prepares a way out, (Verse 65.003) And He provides for him from (sources) he never could imagine. And if any one puts his trust in Allah, sufficient is (Allah) for him. For Allah will surely accomplish his purpose: verily, for all things has Allah appointed a due proportion.

(Verse 65.004) Such of your women as have passed the age of monthly courses, for them the prescribed period, if ye have any doubts, is three months, and for those who have no courses (it is the same): for those who carry (life within their wombs), their period is until they deliver their burdens: and for those who fear Allah, He will make their path easy. (Verse 65.005) That is the Command of Allah, which He has sent down to you: and if any one fears Allah, He will remove his ills, from him, and will enlarge his reward.

(Verse 65.006) Let the women live (in 'iddat) in the same style as ye live, according to your means: Annoy them not, so as to restrict them. And if they carry (life in their wombs), then spend (your substance) on them until they deliver their burden: and if they suckle your (offspring), give them their recompense: and take mutual counsel together, according to what is just and reasonable. And if ye find yourselves in difficulties, let another woman suckle (the child) on the (father's) behalf. (Verse 65.007) Let the man of means spend according to his means: and the man whose resources are restricted, let him spend according to what Allah has given him. Allah puts no burden on any person beyond what He has given him. After a difficulty, Allah will soon grant relief.

Mothers

(Verse 2.233) The mothers shall give such to their offspring for two whole years, if the father desires to complete the term. But he shall bear the cost of their food and clothing on equitable terms. No soul shall have a burden laid on it greater than it can bear. No mother shall be treated unfairly on account of her child. Nor father on account of his child, an heir shall be chargeable in the same way. If they both decide on weaning, by mutual consent, and after due consultation, there is no blame on them. If ye decide on a foster-mother for your offspring, there is no blame on you, provided ye pay (the mother) what ye offered, on equitable terms. But fear Allah and know that Allah sees well what ye do.

(Verse 16.078) It is He Who brought you forth from the wombs of your mothers when ye knew nothing: and He gave you hearing and sight and intelligence and affections: that ye may give thanks (to Allah).

(Verse 31.014) And We have enjoined on man (to be good) to his parents: in travail upon travail did his mother bear him, and in years twain was his weaning: (hear the command), "Show gratitude to Me and to thy parents: to Me is (thy final) Goal. (Verse 31.015) "But if they strive to make thee join in worship with Me things of which thou hast no knowledge, obey them not; yet bear them company in this life with justice (and consideration), and follow the way of those who turn to me (in love): in the end the return of you all is to Me, and I will tell you the truth (and meaning) of all that ye did."

(Verse 46.015) We have enjoined on man kindness to his parents: In pain did his mother bear him, and in pain did she give him birth. The carrying of the (child) to his weaning is (a period of) thirty months. At length, when he reaches the age of full strength and attains forty years, he says, "O my Lord! Grant me that I may be grateful for Thy favor which Thou has bestowed upon me, and upon both my parents, and that I may work righteousness such as Thou mayest approve; and be gracious to me in my issue. Truly have I turned to Thee and truly do I bow (to Thee) in Islam."

(Verse 58.002) If any men among you divorce their wives by Zihar (calling them mothers), they cannot be their mothers: None can be their mothers except those who gave them birth. And in fact they use words (both) iniquitous and false: but truly Allah is one that blots out (sins), and forgives (again and again).

Widows

(Verse 2.234) If any of you die and leave widows behind, they shall wait concerning themselves four months and ten days: When they have fulfilled their term, there is no blame on you if they dispose of themselves in a just and reasonable manner. And Allah is well acquainted with what ye do. (Verse 2.235) There is no blame on you if ye make an offer of betrothal or hold it in your hearts. Allah knows that ye cherish them in your hearts: But do not make a secret contract with them except in terms Honorable, nor resolve on the tie of marriage till the term prescribed is fulfilled. And know that Allah Knoweth what is in your hearts, and take heed of Him; and know that Allah is Oft-forgiving, Most Forbearing.

(Verse 2.240) Those of you who die and leave widows should bequeath for their widows a year's maintenance and residence; but if they leave (The residence), there is no blame on you for what they do with themselves, provided it is reasonable. And Allah is Exalted in Power, Wise.

Parents

(Verse 17.023) Thy Lord hath decreed that ye worship none but Him, and that ye be kind to parents. Whether one or both of them attain old age in thy life, say not to them a word of contempt, nor repel them, but address them in terms of honor. (Verse 17.024) And, out of kindness, lower to them the wing of humility, and say: "My Lord! bestow on them thy Mercy even as they cherished me in childhood."

(Verse 29.008) We have enjoined on man kindness to parents: but if they (either of them) strive (to force) thee to join with Me (in worship) anything of which thou hast no knowledge, obey them not. Ye have (all) to return to me, and I will tell you (the truth) of all that ye did.

(Verse 31.014) And We have enjoined on man (to be good) to his parents: in travail upon travail did his mother bear him, and in years twain was his weaning: (hear the command), "Show gratitude to Me and to thy parents: to Me is (thy final) Goal. (Verse 31.015) "But if they strive to make thee join in worship with Me things of which thou hast no knowledge, obey them not; yet bear them company in this life with justice (and consideration), and follow the way of those who turn to me (in love): in the end the return of you all is to Me, and I will tell you the truth (and meaning) of all that ye did."

(Verse 46.015) We have enjoined on man kindness to his parents: In pain did his mother bear him, and in pain did she give him birth. The carrying of the (child) to his weaning is (a period of) thirty months. At length, when he reaches the age of full strength and attains forty years, he says, "O my Lord! Grant me that I may be grateful for Thy favor which Thou has bestowed upon me, and upon both my parents, and that I may work righteousness such as Thou mayest approve; and be gracious to me in my issue. Truly have I turned to Thee and truly do I bow (to Thee) in Islam."

(Verse 46.017) But (there is one) who says to his parents, "Fie on you! Do ye hold out the promise to me that I shall be raised up, even though generations have passed before me (without rising again)?" And they two seek Allah's aid, (and rebuke the son): "Woe to thee! Have faith! for the promise of Allah is true." But he says, "This is nothing but tales of the ancients!"

Children

(Verse 17.031) Kill not your children for fear of want: We shall provide sustenance for them as well as for you. Verily the killing of them is a great sin.

(Verse 24.058) O ye who believe! let those whom your right hands possess, and the (children) among you who have not come of age ask your permission (before they come to your presence), on three occasions: before morning prayer; the while ye doff your clothes for the noonday heat; and after the late-night prayer: these are your three times of undress: outside those times it is not wrong for you or for them to move about attending to each other: Thus does Allah make clear the Signs to you: for Allah is full of knowledge and wisdom. (Verse 24.059) But when the children among you come of age, let them (also) ask for permission, as do those senior to them (in age): Thus does Allah make clear His Signs to you: for Allah is full of knowledge and wisdom.

(Verse 33.004) Allah has not made for any man two hearts in his (one) body: nor has He made your wives whom ye divorce by Zihar your mothers: nor has He made your adopted sons your sons. Such is (only) your (manner of) speech by your mouths. But Allah tells (you) the Truth, and He shows the (right) Way. (Verse 33.005) Call them by (the names of) their fathers: that is juster in the sight of Allah. But if ye know not their father's (names, call them) your Brothers in faith, or your maulas. But there is no blame on you if ye make a mistake therein: (what counts is) the intention of your hearts: and Allah is Oft-Returning, Most Merciful.

(Verse 42.049) To Allah belongs the dominion of the heavens and the earth.

He creates what He wills (and plans). He bestows (children) male or female according to His Will (and Plan), (Verse 42.050) Or He bestows both males and females, and He leaves barren whom He will: for He is full of Knowledge and Power.

(Verse 90.003) And (the mystic ties of) parent and child;-

Same Sex Relations

(Verse 4.016) If two men among you are guilty of lewdness, punish them both. If they repent and amend, leave them alone; for Allah is Oft-returning, Most Merciful.

(Verse 7.080) We also (sent) Lut: He said to his people: "Do ye commit lewdness such as no people in creation (ever) committed before you? (Verse 7.081) "For ye practice your lusts on men in preference to women: ye are indeed a people transgressing beyond bounds."

(Verse 15.067) The inhabitants of the city came in (mad) joy (at news of the young men). (Verse 15.068) Lut said: "These are my guests: disgrace me not: (Verse 15.069) "But fear Allah, and shame me not." (Verse 15.070) They said: "Did we not forbid thee (to speak) for all and sundry?" (Verse 15.071) He said: "There are my daughters (to marry), if ye must act (so)."

(Verse 26.165) "Of all the creatures in the world, will ye approach males, (Verse 26.166) "And leave those whom Allah has created for you to be your mates? Nay, ye are a people transgressing (all limits)!"

(Verse 27.054) (We also sent) Lut (as a messenger): behold, He said to his people, "Do ye do what is shameful though ye see (its iniquity)? (Verse 27.055) Would ye really approach men in your lusts rather than women? Nay, ye are a people (grossly) ignorant! (Verse 27.056) But his people gave no other answer but this: they said, "Drive out the followers of Lut from your city: these are indeed men who want to be clean and pure!"

(Verse 29.028) And (remember) Lut: behold, he said to his people: "Ye do commit lewdness, such as no people in Creation (ever) committed before you. (Verse 29.029) "Do ye indeed approach men, and cut off the highway?-

and practice wickedness (even) in your councils?" But his people gave no answer but this: they said: "Bring us the Wrath of Allah if thou tellest the truth."

IV

Social Responsibility

Charity

(Verse 2.177) It is not righteousness that ye turn your faces towards East or West; but it is righteousness- to believe in Allah and the Last Day, and the Angels, and the Book, and the Messengers; to spend of your substance, out of love for Him, for your kin, for orphans, for the needy, for the wayfarer, for those who ask, and for the ransom of slaves; to be steadfast in prayer, and practice regular charity; to fulfill the contracts which ye have made; and to be firm and patient, in pain (or suffering) and adversity, and throughout all periods of panic. Such are the people of truth, the Allah-fearing.

(Verse 2.195) And spend of your substance in the cause of Allah, and make not your own hands contribute to (your) destruction; but do good; for Allah loveth those who do good. .

(Verse 2.215) They ask thee what they should spend (In charity). Say: Whatever ye spend that is good, is for parents and kindred and orphans and those in want and for wayfarers. And whatever ye do that is good, -Allah knoweth it well.

(Verse 2.262) Those who spend their substance in the cause of Allah, and follow not up their gifts with reminders of their generosity or with injury,- for them their reward is with their Lord: on them shall be no fear, nor shall they grieve.

(Verse 2.264) O ye who believe! Cancel not your charity by reminders of your generosity or by injury,- like those who spend their substance to be seen of men, but believe neither in Allah nor in the Last Day. They are in parable like a hard, barren rock, on which is a little soil: on it falls heavy rain, which leaves it (Just) a bare stone. They will be able to do nothing with aught they have earned. And Allah guideth not those who reject faith. (Verse 2.265) And the likeness of those who spend their substance, seeking to please Allah and to strengthen their souls, is as a garden, high and fertile: heavy rain falls on it but makes it yield a double increase of harvest, and if it receives not Heavy rain, light moisture sufficeth it. Allah seeth well whatever ye do.

(Verse 2.267) O ye who believe! Give of the good things which ye have (honorably) earned, and of the fruits of the earth which We have produced for you, and do not even aim at getting anything which is bad, in order that out of it ye may give away something, when ye yourselves would not receive it except with closed eyes. And know that Allah is Free of all wants, and worthy of all praise. (Verse 2.268) The Evil one threatens you with poverty and bids you to conduct unseemly. Allah promiseth you His forgiveness and bounties. And Allah careth for all and He knoweth all things.

(Verse 2.270) And whatever ye spend in charity or devotion, be sure Allah knows it all. But the wrong-doers have no helpers. (Verse 2.271) If ye disclose (acts of) charity, even so it is well, but if ye conceal them, and make them reach those (really) in need, that is best for you: It will remove from you some of your (stains of) evil. And Allah is well acquainted with what ye do.

(Verse 2.273) (Charity is) for those in need, who, in Allah's cause are restricted (from travel), and cannot move about in the land, seeking (For trade or work): the ignorant man thinks, because of their modesty, that they are free from want. Thou shalt know them by their (Unfailing) mark: They beg not importunately from all the sundry. And whatever of good ye give, be assured Allah knoweth it well. (Verse 2.274) Those who (in charity) spend of their goods by night and by day, in secret and in public, have their reward with their Lord: on them shall be no fear, nor shall they grieve.

(Verse 3.092) By no means shall ye attain righteousness unless ye give (freely) of that which ye love; and whatever ye give, of a truth Allah knoweth it well.

(Verse 4.036) Serve Allah, and join not any partners with Him; and do good- to parents, kinsfolk, orphans, those in need, neighbors who are near, neighbors who are strangers, the companion by your side, the wayfarer (ye meet), and what your right hands possess: For Allah loveth not the arrogant, the vainglorious;-

(Verse 4.038) Not those who spend of their substance, to be seen of men, but have no faith in Allah and the Last Day: If any take the Evil One for their intimate, what a dreadful intimate he is!

(Verse 9.060) Alms are for the poor and the needy, and those employed to administer the (funds); for those whose hearts have been (recently) reconciled (to Truth); for those in bondage and in debt; in the cause of Allah; and for the wayfarer: (thus is it) ordained by Allah, and Allah is full of knowledge and wisdom.

(Verse 23.060) And those who dispense their charity with their hearts full of fear, because they will return to their Lord;- (Verse 23.061) It is these who hasten in every good work, and these who are foremost in them.

(Verse 30.038) So give what is due to kindred, the needy, and the wayfarer. That is best for those who seek the Countenance, of Allah, and it is they who will prosper. (Verse 30.039) That which ye lay out for increase through the property of (other) people, will have no increase with Allah: but that which ye lay out for charity, seeking the Countenance of Allah, (will increase): it is these who will get a recompense multiplied.

(Verse 47.038) Behold, ye are those invited to spend (of your substance) in the Way of Allah: But among you are some that are niggardly. But any who are niggardly are so at the expense of their own souls. But Allah is free of all wants, and it is ye that are needy. If ye turn back (from the Path), He will substitute in your stead another people; then they would not be like you!

(Verse 57.007) Believe in Allah and His messenger, and spend (in charity) out of the (substance) whereof He has made you heirs. For, those of you who believe and spend (in charity),- for them is a great Reward.

(Verse 57.010) And what cause have ye why ye should not spend in the cause of Allah?- For to Allah belongs the heritage of the heavens and the earth. Not equal among you are those who spent (freely) and fought, before the Victory, (with those who did so later). Those are higher in rank than those who spent (freely) and fought afterwards. But to all has Allah promised a goodly (reward). And Allah is well acquainted with all that ye do.

(Verse 57.018) For those who give in Charity, men and women, and loan to Allah a Beautiful Loan, it shall be increased manifold (to their credit), and they shall have (besides) a liberal reward.

(Verse 58.013) Is it that ye are afraid of spending sums in charity before your private consultation (with him)? If, then, ye do not so, and Allah forgives you, then (at least) establish regular prayer; practise regular charity; and obey Allah and His Messenger. And Allah is well-acquainted with all that ye do.

(Verse 63.010) and spend something (in charity) out of the substance which We have bestowed on you, before Death should come to any of you and he should say, "O my Lord! why didst Thou not give me respite for a little while? I should then have given (largely) in charity, and I should have been one of the doers of good".

(Verse 64.016) So fear Allah as much as ye can; listen and obey and spend in charity for the benefit of your own soul and those saved from the covetousness of their own souls,- they are the ones that achieve prosperity.

(Verse 89.017) Nay, nay! but ye honor not the orphans! (Verse 89.018) Nor do ye encourage one another to feed the poor!- (Verse 89.019) And ye devour inheritance - all with greed, (Verse 89.020) And ye love wealth with inordinate love!

(Verse 93.009) Therefore, treat not the orphan with harshness, (Verse 93.010) Nor repulse the petitioner (unheard); (Verse 93.011) But the bounty of the Lord - rehearse and proclaim!

(Verse 107.002) Then such is the (man) who repulses the orphan (with harshness), (Verse 107.003) And encourages not the feeding of the indigent.

(Verse 107.006) Those who (want but) to be seen (of men), (Verse 107.007) But refuse (to supply) (even) neighborly needs.

Witness, Oaths & Trusts

(Verse 2.224) And make not Allah's (name) an excuse in your oaths against doing good, or acting rightly, or making peace between persons; for Allah is One Who heareth and knoweth all things. (Verse 2.225) Allah will not call you to account for thoughtlessness in your oaths, but for the intention in your hearts; and He is Oft-forgiving, Most Forbearing.

(Verse 4.135) O ye who believe! stand out firmly for justice, as witnesses to Allah, even as against yourselves, or your parents, or your kin, and whether it be (against) rich or poor: for Allah can best protect both. Follow not the lusts (of your hearts), lest ye swerve, and if ye distort (justice) or decline to do justice, verily Allah is well-acquainted with all that ye do.

(Verse 5.089) Allah will not call you to account for what is futile in your oaths, but He will call you to account for your deliberate oaths: for expiation, feed ten indigent persons, on a scale of the average for the food of your families; or clothe them; or give a slave his freedom. If that is beyond your means, fast for three days. That is the expiation for the oaths ye have sworn. But keep to your oaths. Thus doth Allah make clear to you His signs, that ye may be grateful.

(Verse 5.106) O ye who believe! When death approaches any of you, (take) witnesses among yourselves when making bequests,- two just men of your own (brotherhood) or others from outside if ye are journeying through the earth, and the chance of death befalls you (thus). If ye doubt (their truth), detain them both after prayer, and let them both swear by Allah: "We wish not in this for any worldly gain, even though the (beneficiary) be our near relation: we shall hide not the evidence before Allah: if we do, then behold!

the sin be upon us!"

(Verse 5.107) But if it gets known that these two were guilty of the sin (of perjury), let two others stand forth in their places,- nearest in kin from among those who claim a lawful right: let them swear by Allah:

"We affirm that our witness is truer than that of those two, and that we have not trespassed (beyond the truth): if we did, behold! the wrong be upon us!" (Verse 5.108) That is most suitable: that they may give the evidence in its true nature and shape, or else they would fear that other oaths would be taken after their oaths. But fear Allah, and listen (to His counsel): for Allah guideth not a rebellious people: (Verse 5.109) One day will Allah gather the messengers together, and ask: "What was the response ye received (from men to your teaching)?" They will say: "We have no knowledge: it is Thou Who knowest in full all that is hidden."

(Verse 24.011) Those who brought forward the lie are a body among yourselves: think it not to be an evil to you; On the contrary it is good for you: to every man among them (will come the punishment) of the sin that he earned, and to him who took on himself the lead among them, will be a penalty grievous.

(Verse 24.015) Behold, ye received it on your tongues, and said out of your mouths things of which ye had no knowledge; and ye thought it to be a light matter, while it was most serious in the sight of Allah. (Verse 24.016) And why did ye not, when ye heard it, say? - "It is not right of us to speak of this: Glory to Allah! this is a most serious slander!"

(Verse 48.010) Verily those who plight their fealty to thee do no less than plight their fealty to Allah: the Hand of Allah is over their hands: then any one who violates his oath, does so to the harm of his own soul, and any one who fulfils what he has covenanted with Allah,- Allah will soon grant him a great Reward.

(Verse 70.032) And those who respect their trusts and covenants; (Verse 70.033) And those who stand firm in their testimonies.

Preaching & Interpreting

(Verse 9.034) O ye who believe! there are indeed many among the priests and anchorites, who in Falsehood devour the substance of men and hinder (them) from the way of Allah. And there are those who bury gold and silver and spend it not in the way of Allah: announce unto them a most grievous penalty- (Verse 9.035) On the Day when heat will be produced out of that (wealth) in the fire of Hell, and with it will be branded their foreheads, their flanks, and their backs, their flanks, and their backs.- "This is the (treasure) which ye buried for yourselves: taste ye, then, the (treasures) ye buried!"

(Verse 9.107) And there are those who put up a mosque by way of mischief and infidelity - to disunite the Believers - and in preparation for one who warred against Allah and His Messenger aforetime. They will indeed swear that their intention is nothing but good; But Allah doth declare that they are certainly liars. (Verse 9.108) Never stand thou forth therein. There is a mosque whose foundation was laid from the first day on piety; it is more worthy of the standing forth (for prayer) therein. In it are men who love to be purified; and Allah loveth those who make themselves pure.

(Verse 11.018) Who doth more wrong than those who invent a lie against Allah? They will be turned back to the presence of their Lord, and the witnesses will say, "These are the ones who lied against their Lord! Behold! the Curse of Allah is on those who do wrong!- (Verse 11.019) "Those who would hinder (men) from the path of Allah and would seek in it something crooked: these were they who denied the Hereafter!"

(Verse 14.003) Those who love the life of this world more than the Hereafter, who hinder (men) from the Path of Allah and seek therein something crooked: they are astray by a long distance. (Verse 14.004) We sent not a messenger except (to teach) in the language of his (own) people, in order to make (things) clear to them. Now Allah leaves straying those whom He pleases and guides whom He pleases: and He is Exalted in power, full of Wisdom.

(Verse 14.028) Hast thou not turned thy vision to those who have changed the favor of Allah. Into blasphemy and caused their people to descend to the House of Perdition?- (Verse 14.029) Into Hell? They will burn therein,- an evil place to stay in!

(Verse 15.090) (Of just such wrath) as We sent down on those who divided (Scripture into arbitrary parts),- (Verse 15.091) (So also on such) as have made Qur'an into shreds (as they please).

(Verse 16.088) Those who reject Allah and hinder (men) from the Path of Allah - for them will We add Penalty to Penalty; for that they used to spread mischief.

(Verse 16.094) And take not your oaths, to practice deception between yourselves, with the result that someone's foot may slip after it was firmly planted, and ye may have to taste the evil (consequences) of having hindered (men) from the Path of Allah, and a Mighty Wrath descend on you. (Verse 16.095) Nor sell the covenant of Allah for a miserable price: for with Allah is (a prize) far better for you, if ye only knew.

(Verse 16.116) But say not - for any false thing that your tongues may put forth,- "This is lawful, and this is forbidden," so as to ascribe false things to Allah. For those who ascribe false things to Allah, will never prosper.

(Verse 16.125) Invite (all) to the Way of thy Lord with wisdom and beautiful preaching; and argue with them in ways that are best and most gracious: for thy Lord knoweth best, who have strayed from His Path, and who receive guidance.

(Verse 22.071) Yet they worship, besides Allah, things for which no authority has been sent down to them, and of which they have (really) no knowledge: for those that do wrong there is no helper.

(Verse 24.015) Behold, ye received it on your tongues, and said out of your mouths things of which ye had no knowledge; and ye thought it to be a light matter, while it was most serious in the sight of Allah. (Verse 24.016) And why did ye not, when ye heard it, say? - "It is not right of us to speak of this: Glory to Allah! this is a most serious slander!"

(Verse 29.068) And who does more wrong than he who invents a lie against Allah or rejects the Truth when it reaches him? Is there not a home in Hell for those who reject Faith? (Verse 29.069) And those who strive in Our (cause),- We will certainly guide them to our Paths: For verily Allah is with those who do right.

(Verse 30.030) So set thou thy face steadily and truly to the Faith: (establish) Allah's handiwork according to the pattern on which He has made mankind: no change (let there be) in the work (wrought) by Allah: that is the standard Religion: but most among mankind understand not.

(Verse 31.006) But there are, among men, those who purchase idle tales, without knowledge (or meaning), to mislead (men) from the Path of Allah and throw ridicule (on the Path): for such there will be a Humiliating Penalty. (Verse 31.007) When Our Signs are rehearsed to such a one, he turns away in arrogance, as if he heard them not, as if there were deafness in both his ears: announce to him a grievous Penalty.

(Verse 31.021) When they are told to follow the (Revelation) that Allah has sent down, they say: "Nay, we shall follow the ways that we found our fathers (following). "What! even if it is Satan beckoning them to the Penalty of the (Blazing) Fire?

(Verse 33.008) That (Allah) may question the (custodians) of Truth concerning the Truth they (were charged with): And He has prepared for the Unbelievers a grievous Penalty.

(Verse 33.070) O ye who believe! Fear Allah, and (always) say a word directed to the Right:

(Verse 33.071) That He may make your conduct whole and sound and forgive you your sins: He that obeys Allah and His Messenger, has already attained the highest achievement.

(Verse 35.032) Then We have given the Book for inheritance to such of Our Servants as We have chosen: but there are among them some who wrong their own souls; some who follow a middle course; and some who are, by

Allah's leave, foremost in good deeds; that is the highest Grace.

(Verse 39.032) Who, then, doth more wrong than one who utters a lie concerning Allah, and rejects the Truth when it comes to him; is there not in Hell an abode for blasphemers? (Verse 39.033) And he who brings the Truth and he who confirms (and supports) it - such are the men who do right.

(Verse 39.041) Verily We have revealed the Book to thee in Truth, for (instructing) mankind. He, then, that receives guidance benefits his own soul: but he that strays injures his own soul. Nor art thou set over them to dispose of their affairs.

(Verse 39.060) On the Day of Judgment wilt thou see those who told lies against Allah;- their faces will be turned black; Is there not in Hell an abode for the Haughty? (Verse 39.061) But Allah will deliver the righteous to their place of salvation: no evil shall touch them, nor shall they grieve.

(Verse 40.056) Those who dispute about the signs of Allah without any authority bestowed on them,- there is nothing in their breasts but (the quest of) greatness, which they shall never attain to: seek refuge, then, in Allah: It is He Who hears and sees (all things).

(Verse 41.040) Those who pervert the Truth in Our Signs are not hidden from Us. Which is better?- he that is cast into the Fire, or he that comes safe through, on the Day of Judgment? Do what ye will: verily He seeth (clearly) all that ye do.

(Verse 42.018) Only those wish to hasten it who believe not in it: those who believe hold it in awe, and know that it is the Truth. Behold, verily those that dispute concerning the Hour are far astray.

(Verse 42.035) But let those know, who dispute about Our Signs, that there is for them no way of escape.

(Verse 45.017) And We granted them Clear Signs in affairs (of Religion): it was only after knowledge had been granted to them that they fell into schisms, through insolent envy among themselves. Verily thy Lord will judge between them on the Day of Judgment as to those matters in which they set up differences. (Verse 45.018) Then We put thee on the (right) Way of Religion: so follow thou that (Way), and follow not the desires of those who know not.

(Verse 47.016) And among them are men who listen to thee, but in the end, when they go out from thee, they say to those who have received Knowledge, "What is it he said just then?" Such are men whose hearts Allah has sealed, and who follow their own lusts.

(Verse 47.021) Were it to obey and say what is just, and when a matter is resolved on, it were best for them if they were true to Allah.

(Verse 47.024) Do they not then earnestly seek to understand the Qur'an, or are their hearts locked up by them?

(Verse 47.032) Those who reject Allah, hinder (men) from the Path of Allah, and resist the Messenger, after Guidance has been clearly shown to them, will not injure Allah in the least, but He will make their deeds of no effect.

(Verse 47.034) Those who reject Allah, and hinder (men) from the Path of Allah, then die rejecting Allah,- Allah will not forgive them.

(Verse 62.005) The similitude of those who were charged with the (obligations of the) Mosaic Law, but who subsequently failed in those (obligations), is that of a donkey which carries huge tomes (but understands them not). Evil is the similitude of people who falsify the Signs of Allah: and Allah guides not people who do wrong.

(Verse 65.010) Allah has prepared for them a severe Punishment (in the Hereafter). Therefore fear Allah, O ye men of understanding - who have believed!- for Allah hath indeed sent down to you a Message,- (Verse 65.011) An Messenger, who rehearses to you the Signs of Allah containing clear explanations, that he may lead forth those who believe and do righteous deeds from the depths of Darkness into Light. And those who believe in Allah and work righteousness, He will admit to Gardens beneath which Rivers flow, to dwell therein for ever: Allah has indeed granted for them a most excellent Provision.

Building the Community

(Verse 2.150) So from whencesoever Thou startest forth, turn Thy face in the direction of the sacred Mosque; and wheresoever ye are, Turn your face thither: that there be no ground of dispute against you among the people, except those of them that are bent on wickedness; so fear them not, but fear Me; and that I may complete My favours on you, and ye May (consent to) be guided;

(Verse 3.200) O ye who believe! Persevere in patience and constancy; vie in such perseverance; strengthen each other; and fear Allah; that ye may prosper.

(Verse 5.055) Your (real) friends are (no less than) Allah, His Messenger, and the (fellowship of) believers,- those who establish regular prayers and regular charity, and they bow down humbly (in worship).

(Verse 6.038) There is not an animal (that lives) on the earth, nor a being that flies on its wings, but (forms part of) communities like you. Nothing have we omitted from the Book, and they (all) shall be gathered to their Lord in the end.

(Verse 8.046) And obey Allah and His Messenger; and fall into no disputes, lest ye lose heart and your power depart; and be patient and persevering: For Allah is with those who patiently persevere: (Verse 8.047) And be not like those who started from their homes insolently and to be seen of men, and to hinder (men) from the path of Allah: For Allah compasseth round about all that they do.

(Verse 13.011) For each (such person) there are (angels) in succession, before and behind him: They guard him by command of Allah. Allah does not change a people's lot unless they change what is in their hearts. But when (once) Allah willeth a people's punishment, there can be no turning it back, nor will they find, besides Him, any to protect.

(Verse 16.092) And be not like a woman who breaks into untwisted strands the yarn which she has spun, after it has become strong. Nor take your oaths to practice deception between yourselves, lest one party should be more numerous than another: for Allah will test you by this; and on the Day of Judgment He will certainly make clear to you (the truth of) that wherein ye disagree.

(Verse 17.016) When We decide to destroy a population, We (first) send a definite order to those among them who are given the good things of this life and yet transgress; so that the word is proved true against them: then (it is) We destroy them utterly.

(Verse 17.053) Say to My servants that they should (only) say those things that are best: for Satan doth sow dissensions among them: For Satan is to man an avowed enemy.

(Verse 19.069) Then shall We certainly drag out from every sect all those who were worst in obstinate rebellion against (Allah) Most Gracious.

(Verse 30.032) Those who split up their Religion, and become (mere) Sects,- each party rejoicing in that which is with itself! (Verse 30.033) When trouble touches men, they cry to their Lord, turning back to Him in repentance: but when He gives them a taste of Mercy as from Himself, behold, some of them pay part- worship to other god's besides their Lord,- (Verse 30.034) (As if) to show their ingratitude for the (favors) We have bestowed on them! Then enjoy (your brief day); but soon will ye know (your folly). (Verse 30.035) Or have We sent down authority to them, which points out to them the things to which they pay part- worship?

(Verse 30.041) Mischief has appeared on land and sea because of (the meed) that the hands of men have earned, that (Allah) may give them a taste of some of their deeds: in order that they may turn back (from Evil).

(Verse 33.006) The Prophet is closer to the Believers than their own selves, and his wives are their mothers. Blood-relations among each other have closer personal ties, in the Decree of Allah. Than (the Brotherhood of)

Believers and Muhajirs: nevertheless do ye what is just to your closest friends: such is the writing in the Decree (of Allah).

(Verse 37.001) By those who range themselves in ranks, (Verse 37.002) And so are strong in repelling (evil), (Verse 37.003) And thus proclaim the Message (of Allah)!

(Verse 45.028) And thou wilt see every sect bowing the knee: Every sect will be called to its Record: "This Day shall ye be recompensed for all that ye did!

(Verse 49.007) And know that among you is Allah's Messenger: were he, in many matters, to follow your (wishes), ye would certainly fall into misfortune: But Allah has endeared the Faith to you, and has made it beautiful in your hearts, and He has made hateful to you Unbelief, wickedness, and rebellion: such indeed are those who walk in righteousness;-

(Verse 49.009) If two parties among the Believers fall into a quarrel, make ye peace between them: but if one of them transgresses beyond bounds against the other, then fight ye (all) against the one that transgresses until it complies with the command of Allah; but if it complies, then make peace between them with justice, and be fair: for Allah loves those who are fair (and just).

(Verse 58.011) O ye who believe! When ye are told to make room in the assemblies, (spread out and) make room: (ample) room will Allah provide for you. And when ye are told to rise up, rise up Allah will rise up, to (suitable) ranks (and degrees), those of you who believe and who have been granted (mystic) Knowledge. And Allah is well-acquainted with all ye do.

Privacy & Transparency

(Verse 2.189) They ask thee concerning the New Moons. Say: They are but signs to mark fixed periods of time in (the affairs of) men, and for Pilgrimage. It is no virtue if ye enter your houses from the back: It is virtue if ye fear Allah. Enter houses through the proper doors: And fear Allah: That ye may prosper.

(Verse 2.263) Kind words and the covering of faults are better than charity followed by injury. Allah is free of all wants, and He is Most-Forbearing.

(Verse 24.019) Those who love (to see) scandal published broadcast among the Believers, will have a grievous Penalty in this life and in the Hereafter: Allah knows, and ye know not.

(Verse 24.027) O ye who believe! enter not houses other than your own, until ye have asked permission and saluted those in them: that is best for you, in order that ye may heed (what is seemly). (Verse 24.028) If ye find no one in the house, enter not until permission is given to you: if ye are asked to go back, go back: that makes for greater purity for yourselves: and Allah knows well all that ye do. (Verse 24.029) It is no fault on your part to enter houses not used for living in, which serve some (other) use for you: And Allah has knowledge of what ye reveal and what ye conceal.

(Verse 49.006) O ye who believe! If a wicked person comes to you with any news, ascertain the truth, lest ye harm people unwittingly, and afterwards become full of repentance for what ye have done.

(Verse 49.012) O ye who believe! Avoid suspicion as much (as possible): for suspicion in some cases is a sin: And spy not on each other behind their backs. Would any of you like to eat the flesh of his dead brother? Nay, ye would abhor it... But fear Allah: For Allah is Oft-Returning, Most Merciful.

(Verse 58.007) Seest thou not that Allah doth know (all) that is in the heavens and on earth? There is not a secret consultation between three, but He makes the fourth among them, - Nor between five but He makes the sixth,- nor between fewer nor more, but He is in their midst, wheresoever they be: In the end will He tell them the truth of their conduct, on the Day of Judgment. For Allah has full knowledge of all things. (Verse 58.008) Turnest thou not thy sight towards those who were forbidden secret counsels yet revert to that which they were forbidden (to do)? And they hold secret counsels among themselves for iniquity and hostility, and disobedience to the Messenger. And when they come to thee, they salute thee, not as Allah salutes thee, (but in crooked ways): And they say to themselves, "Why does not Allah punish us for our words?" Enough for them is Hell: In it will they burn, and evil is that destination! (Verse 58.009) O ye who believe! When ye hold secret counsel, do it not for iniquity and hostility, and disobedience to the Prophet; but do it for righteousness and self-restraint; and fear Allah, to Whom ye shall be brought back.

(Verse 58.010) Secret counsels are only (inspired) by the Evil One, in order that he may cause grief to the Believers; but he cannot harm them in the least, except as Allah permits; and on Allah let the Believers put their trust.

(Verse 104.001) Woe to every (kind of) scandal-monger and- backbiter,
Disable

(Verse 24.061) It is no fault in the blind nor in one born lame, nor in one afflicted with illness, nor in yourselves, that ye should eat in your own houses, or those of your fathers, or your mothers, or your brothers, or your sisters, or your father's brothers or your father's sisters, or your mother's brothers, or your mother's sisters, or in houses of which the keys are in your possession, or in the house of a sincere friend of yours: there is no blame on you, whether ye eat in company or separately. But if ye enter houses, salute each other - a greeting of blessing and purity as from Allah. Thus does Allah make clear the signs to you: that ye may understand.

(Verse 80.001) (The Prophet) frowned and turned away, (Verse 80.002) Because there came to him the blind man (interrupting). (Verse 80.003)

But what could tell thee but that perchance he might grow (in spiritual understanding)?- (Verse 80.004) Or that he might receive admonition, and the teaching might profit him? (Verse 80.005) As to one who regards Himself as self-sufficient, (Verse 80.006) To him dost thou attend; (Verse 80.007) Though it is no blame to thee if he grow not (in spiritual understanding). (Verse 80.008) But as to him who came to thee striving earnestly, (Verse 80.009) And with fear (in his heart), (Verse 80.010) Of him wast thou unmindful.

Law & Order

(Verse 2.011) When it is said to them: "Make not mischief on the earth," they say: "Why, we only Want to make peace!"

(Verse 2.084) And remember We took your covenant (to this effect): Shed no blood amongst you, nor turn out your own people from your homes: and this ye solemnly ratified, and to this ye can bear witness.

(Verse 2.205) When he turns his back, His aim everywhere is to spread mischief through the earth and destroy crops and cattle. But Allah loveth not mischief. (Verse 2.206) When it is said to him, "Fear Allah", He is led by arrogance to (more) crime. Enough for him is Hell;-An evil bed indeed (To lie on)!

(Verse 7.056) Do no mischief on the earth, after it hath been set in order, but call on Him with fear and longing (in your hearts): for the Mercy of Allah is (always) near to those who do good.

(Verse 16.090) Allah commands justice, the doing of good, and liberality to kith and kin, and He forbids all shameful deeds, and injustice and rebellion: He instructs you, that ye may receive admonition.

(Verse 17.033) Nor take life - which Allah has made sacred - except for just cause. And if anyone is slain wrongfully, we have given his heir authority (to demand qisas or to forgive): but let him not exceed bounds in the matter of taking life; for he is helped (by the Law).

(Verse 33.060) Truly, if the Hypocrites, and those in whose hearts is a disease, and those who stir up sedition in the City, desist not, We shall certainly stir thee up against them: Then will they not be able to stay in it as thy neighbors for any length of time: (Verse 33.061) They shall have a curse on them: whenever they are found, they shall be seized and slain (without mercy).

(Verse 42.042) The blame is only against those who oppress men and wrong-doing and insolently transgress beyond bounds through the land, defying right and justice: for such there will be a penalty grievous. (Verse 42.043) But indeed if any show patience and forgive, that would truly be an exercise of courageous will and resolution in the conduct of affairs.

V

Organizing Society

Sovereignty

(Verse 2.107) Knowest thou not that to Allah belongeth the dominion of the heavens and the earth? And besides Him ye have neither patron nor helper.

(Verse 2.115) To Allah belong the East and the West: Whithersoever ye turn, there is the presence of Allah. For Allah is all-Pervading, all-Knowing.

(Verse 2.117) To Him is due the primal origin of the heavens and the earth: When He decreeth a matter, He saith to it: "Be," and it is.

(Verse 6.012) Say: "To whom belongeth all that is in the heavens and on earth?" Say: "To Allah. He hath inscribed for Himself (the rule of) Mercy. That He will gather you together for the Day of Judgment, there is no doubt whatever. It is they who have lost their own souls, that will not believe. (Verse 6.013) To him belongeth all that dwelleth (or lurketh) in the night and the day. For he is the one who heareth and knoweth all things."

(Verse 7.054) Your Guardian-Lord is Allah, Who created the heavens and the earth in six days, and is firmly established on the throne (of authority): He draweth the night as a veil o'er the day, each seeking the other in rapid succession: He created the sun, the moon, and the stars, (all) governed by laws under His command. Is it not His to create and to govern? Blessed be Allah, the Cherisher and Sustainer of the worlds!

(Verse 7.185) Do they see nothing in the government of the heavens and the earth and all that Allah hath created? (Do they not see) that it may well be that their terms is nigh drawing to an end? In what message after this will they then believe?

(Verse 9.116) Unto Allah belongeth the dominion of the heavens and the earth. He giveth life and He taketh it. Except for Him ye have no protector nor helper.

(Verse 10.003) Verily your Lord is Allah, who created the heavens and the earth in six days, and is firmly established on the throne (of authority), regulating and governing all things. No intercessor (can plead with Him) except after His leave (hath been obtained). This is Allah your Lord; Him therefore serve ye: will ye not receive admonition?

(Verse 10.055) Is it not (the case) that to Allah belongeth whatever is in the heavens and on earth? Is it not (the case) that Allah's promise is assuredly true? Yet most of them understand not. (Verse 10.056) It is He Who giveth life and who taketh it, and to Him shall ye all be brought back.

(Verse 10.066) Behold! verily to Allah belong all creatures, in the heavens and on earth. What do they follow who worship as His "partners" other than Allah? They follow nothing but fancy, and they do nothing but lie.

(Verse 13.002) Allah is He Who raised the heavens without any pillars that ye can see; is firmly established on the throne (of authority); He has subjected the sun and the moon (to his Law)! Each one runs (its course) for a term appointed. He doth regulate all affairs, explaining the signs in detail, that ye may believe with certainty in the meeting with your Lord.

(Verse 14.002) Of Allah, to Whom do belong all things in the heavens and on earth! But alas for the Unbelievers for a terrible penalty (their Unfaith will bring them)!- (Verse 14.003) Those who love the life of this world more than the Hereafter, who hinder (men) from the Path of Allah and seek therein something crooked: they are astray by a long distance.

(Verse 15.023) And verily, it is We Who give life, and Who give death: it is We Who remain inheritors (after all else passes away).

(Verse 16.052) To Him belongs whatever is in the heavens and on earth, and to Him is duty due always: then will ye fear other than Allah?

(Verse 21.019) To Him belong all (creatures) in the heavens and on earth: Even those who are in His (very) Presence are not too proud to serve Him, nor are they (ever) weary (of His service):

(Verse 23.088) Say: "Who is it in whose hands is the governance of all things,- who protects (all), but is not protected (of any)? (say) if ye know." (Verse 23.089) They will say, "(It belongs) to Allah." Say: "Then how are ye deluded?"

(Verse 24.042) Yea, to Allah belongs the dominion of the heavens and the earth; and to Allah is the final goal (of all).

(Verse 25.001) Blessed is He who sent down the criterion to His servant, that it may be an admonition to all creatures;- (Verse 25.002) He to whom belongs the dominion of the heavens and the earth: no son has He begotten, nor has He a partner in His dominion: it is He who created all things, and ordered them in due proportions.

(Verse 25.059) He Who created the heavens and the earth and all that is between, in six days, and is firmly established on the Throne (of Authority): Allah Most Gracious: ask thou, then, about Him of any acquainted (with such things).

(Verse 32.004) It is Allah Who has created the heavens and the earth, and all between them, in six Days, and is firmly established on the Throne (of Authority): ye have none, besides Him, to protect or intercede (for you): will ye not then receive admonition? (Verse 32.005) He rules (all) affairs from the heavens to the earth: in the end will (all affairs) go up to Him, on a Day, the space whereof will be (as) a thousand years of your reckoning.

(Verse 43.082) Glory to the Lord of the heavens and the earth, the Lord of the Throne (of Authority)! (He is free) from the things they attribute (to him)!

(Verse 45.027) To Allah belongs the dominion of the heavens and the earth, and the Day that the Hour of Judgment is established,- that Day will the dealers in Falsehood perish!

(Verse 57.002) To Him belongs the dominion of the heavens and the earth: It is He Who gives Life and Death; and He has Power over all things.

(Verse 59.023) Allah is He, than Whom there is no other god;- the Sovereign, the Holy One, the Source of Peace (and Perfection), the Guardian of Faith, the Preserver of Safety, the Exalted in Might, the Irresistible, the Supreme: Glory to Allah! (High is He) above the partners they attribute to Him. (Verse 59.024) He is Allah, the Creator, the Evolver, the Bestower of Forms (or Colours). To Him belong the Most Beautiful Names: whatever is in the heavens and on earth, doth declare His Praises and Glory: and He is the Exalted in Might, the Wise.

(Verse 62.001) Whatever is in the heavens and on earth, doth declare the Praises and Glory of Allah,- the Sovereign, the Holy One, the Exalted in Might, the Wise.

(Verse 67.001) Blessed be He in Whose hands is Dominion; and He over all things hath Power;- (Verse 67.002) He Who created Death and Life, that He may try which of you is best in deed: and He is the Exalted in Might, Oft-Forgiving;- (Verse 67.003) He Who created the seven heavens one above another: No want of proportion wilt thou see in the Creation of (Allah) Most Gracious. So turn thy vision again: seest thou any flaw? (Verse 67.004) Again turn thy vision a second time: (thy) vision will come back to thee dull and discomfited, in a state worn out.

Ummah & Cultures

(Verse 2.143) Thus, have We made of you an Ummat justly balanced, that ye might be witnesses over the nations, and the Messenger a witness over yourselves; and We appointed the Qibla to which thou wast used, only to test those who followed the Messenger from those who would turn on their heels (From the Faith). Indeed it was (A change) momentous, except to those guided by Allah. And never would Allah Make your faith of no effect. For Allah is to all people Most surely full of kindness, Most Merciful.

(Verse 2.148) To each is a goal to which Allah turns him; then strive together (as in a race) Towards all that is good. Wheresoever ye are, Allah will bring you Together. For Allah Hath power over all things. (Verse 2.149) From whencesoever Thou startest forth, turn Thy face in the direction of the sacred Mosque; that is indeed the truth from the Lord. And Allah is not unmindful of what ye do.

(Verse 3.103) And hold fast, all together, by the rope which Allah (stretches out for you), and be not divided among yourselves; and remember with gratitude Allah's favour on you; for ye were enemies and He joined your hearts in love, so that by His Grace, ye became brethren; and ye were on the brink of the pit of Fire, and He saved you from it. Thus doth Allah make His Signs clear to you: That ye may be guided. (Verse 3.104) Let there arise out of you a band of people inviting to all that is good, enjoining what is right, and forbidding what is wrong: They are the ones to attain felicity. (Verse 3.105) Be not like those who are divided amongst themselves and fall into disputations after receiving Clear Signs: For them is a dreadful penalty,-

(Verse 3.110) Ye are the best of peoples, evolved for mankind, enjoining what is right, forbidding what is wrong, and believing in Allah. If only the People of the Book had faith, it were best for them: among them are some who have faith, but most of them are perverted transgressors.

(Verse 6.159) As for those who divide their religion and break up into sects, thou hast no part in them in the least: their affair is with Allah: He will in the end tell them the truth of all that they did.

(Verse 7.168) We broke them up into sections on this earth. There are among them some that are the righteous, and some that are the opposite. We have tried them with both prosperity and adversity: In order that they might turn (to us). (Verse 7.169) After them succeeded an (evil) generation: They inherited the Book, but they chose (for themselves) the vanities of this world, saying (for excuse): "(Everything) will be forgiven us." (Even so), if similar vanities came their way, they would (again) seize them. Was not the covenant of the Book taken from them, that they would not ascribe to Allah anything but the truth? and they study what is in the Book. But best for the righteous is the home in the Hereafter. Will ye not understand?

(Verse 10.019) Mankind was but one nation, but differed (later). Had it not been for a word that went forth before from thy Lord, their differences would have been settled between them.

(Verse 11.017) Can they be (like) those who accept a Clear (Sign) from their Lord, and whom a witness from Himself doth teach, as did the Book of Moses before it,- a guide and a mercy? They believe therein; but those of the Sects that reject it,- the Fire will be their promised meeting-place. Be not then in doubt thereon: for it is the truth from thy Lord: yet many among men do not believe!

(Verse 11.118) If thy Lord had so willed, He could have made mankind one people: but they will not cease to dispute.

(Verse 16.093) If Allah so willed, He could make you all one people: But He leaves straying whom He pleases, and He guides whom He pleases: but ye shall certainly be called to account for all your actions.

(Verse 21.092) Verily, this brotherhood of yours is a single brotherhood, and I am your Lord and Cherisher: therefore serve Me (and no other).

(Verse 21.093) But (later generations) cut off their affair (of unity), one from another: (yet) will they all return to Us.

(Verse 22.067) To every People have We appointed rites and ceremonies which they must follow: let them not then dispute with thee on the matter, but do thou invite (them) to thy Lord: for thou art assuredly on the Right Way.

(Verse 23.052) And verily this Brotherhood of yours is a single Brotherhood, and I am your Lord and Cherisher: therefore fear Me (and no other). (Verse 23.053) But people have cut off their affair (of unity), between them, into sects: each party rejoices in that which is with itself.

(Verse 23.079) And He has multiplied you through the earth, and to Him shall ye be gathered back.

(Verse 30.022) And among His Signs is the creation of the heavens and the earth, and the variations in your languages and your colors: verily in that are Signs for those who know.

(Verse 42.008) If Allah had so willed, He could have made them a single people; but He admits whom He will to His Mercy; and the Wrong-doers will have no protector nor helper.

(Verse 42.013) The same religion has He established for you as that which He enjoined on Noah - the which We have sent by inspiration to thee - and that which We enjoined on Abraham, Moses, and Jesus: Namely, that ye should remain steadfast in religion, and make no divisions therein: to those who worship other things than Allah, hard is the (way) to which thou callest them. Allah chooses to Himself those whom He pleases, and guides to Himself those who turn (to Him). (Verse 42.014) And they became divided only after Knowledge reached them,- through selfish envy as between themselves. Had it not been for a Word that went forth before from thy Lord, (tending) to a Term appointed, the matter would have been settled between them: But truly those who have inherited the Book after them are in suspicious (disquieting) doubt concerning it.

(Verse 49.013) O mankind! We created you from a single (pair) of a male and a female, and made you into nations and tribes, that ye may know each other (not that ye may despise (each other). Verily the most honored of you in the sight of Allah is (he who is) the most righteous of you. And Allah has full knowledge and is well acquainted (with all things).

Leaders

(Verse 3.026) Say: "O Allah! Lord of Power (And Rule), Thou givest power to whom Thou pleasest, and Thou strippest off power from whom Thou pleasest: Thou enduest with honour whom Thou pleasest, and Thou bringest low whom Thou pleasest: In Thy hand is all good. Verily, over all things Thou hast power. (Verse 3.027) "Thou causest the night to gain on the day, and thou causest the day to gain on the night; Thou bringest the Living out of the dead, and Thou bringest the dead out of the Living; and Thou givest sustenance to whom Thou pleasest, without measure."

(Verse 3.104) Let there arise out of you a band of people inviting to all that is good, enjoining what is right, and forbidding what is wrong: they are the ones to attain felicity. (Verse 3.105) Be not like those who are divided amongst themselves and fall into disputations after receiving Clear Signs: For them is a dreadful penalty,-

(Verse 4.059) O ye who believe! Obey Allah, and obey the Messenger, and those charged with authority among you. If ye differ in anything among yourselves, refer it to Allah and His Messenger, if ye do believe in Allah and the Last Day: That is best, and most suitable for final determination.

(Verse 4.083) When there comes to them some matter touching (Public) safety or fear, they divulge it. If they had only referred it to the Messenger, or to those charged with authority among them, the proper investigators would have Tested it from them (direct). Were it not for the Grace and Mercy of Allah unto you, all but a few of you would have fallen into the clutches of Satan.

(Verse 4.148) Allah loveth not that evil should be noised abroad in public speech, except where injustice hath been done; for Allah is He who heareth and knoweth all things. (Verse 4.149) Whether ye publish a good deed or conceal it or cover evil with pardon, verily Allah doth blot out (sins) and hath power (in the judgment of values).

(Verse 6.123) Thus have We placed leaders in every town, its wicked men, to plot (and burrow) therein: but they only plot against their own souls, and they perceive it not.

(Verse 6.165) It is He Who hath made you (His) agents, inheritors of the earth: He hath raised you in ranks, some above others: that He may try you in the gifts He hath given you: for thy Lord is quick in punishment: yet He is indeed Oft-forgiving, Most Merciful.

(Verse 7.181) Of those We have created are people who direct (others) with truth. And dispense justice therewith.

(Verse 9.040) If ye help not (your leader), (it is no matter): for Allah did indeed help him, when the Unbelievers drove him out: he had no more than one companion; they two were in the cave, and he said to his companion, "Have no fear, for Allah is with us": then Allah sent down His peace upon him, and strengthened him with forces which ye saw not, and humbled to the depths the word of the Unbelievers. But the word of Allah is exalted to the heights: for Allah is Exalted in might, Wise.

(Verse 11.116) Why were there not, among the generations before you, persons possessed of balanced good sense, prohibiting (men) from mischief in the earth - except a few among them whom We saved (from harm)? But the wrong-doers pursued the enjoyment of the good things of life which were given them, and persisted in sin. (Verse 11.117) Nor would thy Lord be the One to destroy communities for a single wrong-doing, if its members were likely to mend. (Verse 11.118) If thy Lord had so willed, He could have made mankind one people: but they will not cease to dispute.

(Verse 24.055) Allah has promised, to those among you who believe and work righteous deeds, that He will, of a surety, grant them in the land, inheritance (of power), as He granted it to those before them; that He will establish in authority their religion - the one which He has chosen for them; and that He will change (their state), after the fear in which they (lived), to one of security and peace: 'They will worship Me (alone) and not associate aught with Me. 'If any do reject Faith after this, they are rebellious and wicked.

(Verse 47.022) Then, is it to be expected of you, if ye were put in authority, that ye will do mischief in the land, and break your ties of kith and kin? (Verse 47.023) Such are the men whom Allah has cursed for He has made them deaf and blinded their sight.

Legislation

(Verse 6.165) It is He Who hath made you (His) agents, inheritors of the earth: He hath raised you in ranks, some above others: that He may try you in the gifts He hath given you: for thy Lord is quick in punishment: yet He is indeed Oft-forgiving, Most Merciful.

(Verse 7.010) It is We Who have placed you with authority on earth, and provided you therein with means for the fulfillment of your life: small are the thanks that ye give!

(Verse 7.128) Said Moses to his people: "Pray for help from Allah, and (wait) in patience and constancy: for the earth is Allah's, to give as a heritage to such of His servants as He pleaseth; and the end is (best) for the righteous.

(Verse 33.036) It is not fitting for a Believer, man or woman, when a matter has been decided by Allah and His Messenger to have any option about their decision: if any one disobeys Allah and His Messenger, he is indeed on a clearly wrong Path.

(Verse 35.039) He it is That has made you inheritors in the earth: if, then, any do reject (Allah), their rejection (works) against themselves: their rejection but adds to the odium for the Unbelievers in the sight of their Lord: their rejection but adds to (their own) undoing.

(Verse 38.026) O David! We did indeed make thee a vicegerent on earth: so judge thou between men in truth (and justice): Nor follow thou the lusts (of thy heart), for they will mislead thee from the Path of Allah: for those who wander astray from the Path of Allah, is a Penalty Grievous, for that they forget the Day of Account.

(Verse 42.038) Those who hearken to their Lord, and establish regular

Prayer; who (conduct) their affairs by mutual Consultation; who spend out of what We bestow on them for Sustenance;

Justice

(Verse 2.188) And do not eat up your property among yourselves for vanities, nor use it as bait for the judges, with intent that ye may eat up wrongfully and knowingly a little of (other) people's property.

(Verse 3.018) There is no god but He: That is the witness of Allah, His angels, and those endued with knowledge, standing firm on justice. There is no god but He, the Exalted in Power, the Wise.

(Verse 4.058) Allah doth command you to render back your Trusts to those to whom they are due; And when ye judge between man and man, that ye judge with justice: Verily how excellent is the teaching which He giveth you! For Allah is He Who heareth and seeth all things.

(Verse 4.065) But no, by the Lord, they can have no (real) Faith, until they make thee judge in all disputes between them, and find in their souls no resistance against Thy decisions, but accept them with the fullest conviction.

(Verse 4.105) We have sent down to thee the Book in truth, that thou mightest judge between men, as guided by Allah: so be not (used) as an advocate by those who betray their trust; (Verse 4.106) But seek the forgiveness of Allah; for Allah is Oft-forgiving, Most Merciful.

(Verse 5.008) O ye who believe! stand out firmly for Allah, as witnesses to fair dealing, and let not the hatred of others to you make you swerve to wrong and depart from justice. Be just: that is next to piety: and fear Allah. For Allah is well-acquainted with all that ye do.

(Verse 5.042) (They are fond of) listening to falsehood, of devouring anything forbidden. If they do come to thee, either judge between them, or decline to interfere. If thou decline, they cannot hurt thee in the least. If thou judge, judge in equity between them. For Allah loveth those who judge in equity.

(Verse 5.043) But why do they come to thee for decision, when they have (their own) law before them?- therein is the (plain) command of Allah; yet even after that, they would turn away. For they are not (really) People of Faith. (Verse 5.044) It was We who revealed the law (to Moses): therein was guidance and light. By its standard have been judged the Jews, by the prophets who bowed (as in Islam) to Allah's will, by the rabbis and the doctors of law: for to them was entrusted the protection of Allah's book, and they were witnesses thereto: therefore fear not men, but fear me, and sell not my signs for a miserable price. If any do fail to judge by (the light of) what Allah hath revealed, they are (no better than) Unbelievers. (Verse 5.045) We ordained therein for them: "Life for life, eye for eye, nose or nose, ear for ear, tooth for tooth, and wounds equal for equal." But if any one remits the retaliation by way of charity, it is an act of atonement for himself. And if any fail to judge by (the light of) what Allah hath revealed, they are (No better than) wrong-doers.

(Verse 5.046) And in their footsteps We sent Jesus the son of Mary, confirming the Law that had come before him: We sent him the Gospel: therein was guidance and light, and confirmation of the Law that had come before him: a guidance and an admonition to those who fear Allah. (Verse 5.047) Let the people of the Gospel judge by what Allah hath revealed therein. If any do fail to judge by (the light of) what Allah hath revealed, they are (no better than) those who rebel.

(Verse 5.048) To thee We sent the Scripture in truth, confirming the scripture that came before it, and guarding it in safety: so judge between them by what Allah hath revealed, and follow not their vain desires, diverging from the Truth that hath come to thee. To each among you have we prescribed a law and an open way. If Allah had so willed, He would have made you a single people, but (His plan is) to test you in what He hath given you: so strive as in a race in all virtues. The goal of you all is to Allah; it is He that will show you the truth of the matters in which ye dispute;

(Verse 5.049) And this (He commands): Judge thou between them by what

Allah hath revealed, and follow not their vain desires, but beware of them lest they beguile thee from any of that (teaching) which Allah hath sent down to thee. And if they turn away, be assured that for some of their crime it is Allah's purpose to punish them. And truly most men are rebellious.

(Verse 6.115) The word of thy Lord doth find its fulfillment in truth and in justice: None can change His words: for He is the one who heareth and knoweth all.

(Verse 8.029) O ye who believe! if ye fear Allah, He will grant you a criterion (to judge between right and wrong), remove from you (all) evil (that may afflict) you, and forgive you: for Allah is the Lord of grace unbounded.

(Verse 16.076) Allah sets forth (another) Parable of two men: one of them dumb, with no power of any sort; a wearisome burden is he to his master; whichever way be directs him, he brings no good: is such a man equal with one who commands Justice, and is on a Straight Way?

(Verse 35.018) Nor can a bearer of burdens bear another's burdens if one heavily laden should call another to (bear) his load. Not the least portion of it can be carried (by the other). Even though he be nearly related. Thou canst but admonish such as fear their Lord unseen and establish regular Prayer. And whoever purifies himself does so for the benefit of his own soul; and the destination (of all) is to Allah.

(Verse 39.007) If ye reject (Allah), Truly Allah hath no need of you; but He liketh not ingratitude from His servants: if ye are grateful, He is pleased with you. No bearer of burdens can bear the burden of another. In the end, to your Lord is your Return, when He will tell you the truth of all that ye did (in this life). for He knoweth well all that is in (men's) hearts.

(Verse 39.069) And the Earth will shine with the Glory of its Lord: the Record (of Deeds) will be placed (open); the prophets and the witnesses will be brought forward and a just decision pronounced between them; and they will not be wronged (in the least).

(Verse 40.020) And Allah will judge with (justice and) Truth: but those whom (men) invoke besides Him, will not (be in a position) to judge at all. Verily it is Allah (alone) Who hears and sees (all things).

(Verse 42.040) The recompense for an injury is an injury equal thereto (in degree): but if a person forgives and makes reconciliation, his reward is due from Allah: for (Allah) loveth not those who do wrong. (Verse 42.041) But indeed if any do help and defend themselves after a wrong (done) to them, against such there is no cause of blame. (Verse 42.042) The blame is only against those who oppress men and wrong-doing and insolently transgress beyond bounds through the land, defying right and justice: for such there will be a penalty grievous.

(Verse 45.022) Allah created the heavens and the earth for just ends, and in order that each soul may find the recompense of what it has earned, and none of them be wronged.

(Verse 46.019) And to all are (assigned) degrees according to the deeds which they (have done), and in order that (Allah) may recompense their deeds, and no injustice be done to them.

(Verse 51.006) And verily Judgment and Justice must indeed come to pass.

(Verse 53.038) Namely, that no bearer of burdens can bear the burden of another; (Verse 53.039) That man can have nothing but what he strives for; (Verse 53.040) That (the fruit of) his striving will soon come in sight: (Verse 53.041) Then will he be rewarded with a reward complete;

Crime & Punishment

Adultery

(Verse 4.015) If any of your women are guilty of lewdness, Take the evidence of four (Reliable) witnesses from amongst you against them; and if they testify, confine them to houses until death do claim them, or Allah ordain for them some (other) way.

(Verse 4.016) If two men among you are guilty of lewdness, punish them both. If they repent and amend, Leave them alone; for Allah is Oft-returning, Most Merciful.

(Verse 24.002) The woman and the man guilty of adultery or fornication,- flog each of them with a hundred stripes: Let not compassion move you in their case, in a matter prescribed by Allah, if ye believe in Allah and the Last Day: and let a party of the Believers witness their punishment. (Verse 24.003) Let no man guilty of adultery or fornication marry and but a woman similarly guilty, or an Unbeliever: nor let any but such a man or an Unbeliever marry such a woman: to the Believers such a thing is forbidden.

(Verse 24.004) And those who launch a charge against chaste women, and produce not four witnesses (to support their allegations),- flog them with eighty stripes; and reject their evidence ever after: for such men are wicked transgressors;- (Verse 24.005) Unless they repent thereafter and mend (their conduct); for Allah is Oft-Forgiving, Most Merciful. (Verse 24.006) And for those who launch a charge against their spouses, and have (in support) no evidence but their own,- their solitary evidence (can be received) if they bear witness four times (with an oath) by Allah that they are solemnly telling the truth; (Verse 24.007) And the fifth (oath) (should be) that they solemnly invoke the curse of Allah on themselves if they tell a lie.

(Verse 24.008) But it would avert the punishment from the wife, if she bears witness four times (with an oath) By Allah, that (her husband) is telling a lie; (Verse 24.009) And the fifth (oath) should be that she solemnly invokes the wrath of Allah on herself if (her accuser) is telling the truth.

(Verse 24.012) Why did not the believers - men and women - when ye heard of the affair,- put the best construction on it in their own minds and say, "This (charge) is an obvious lie"? (Verse 24.013) Why did they not bring four witnesses to prove it? When they have not brought the witnesses, such men, in the sight of Allah, (stand forth) themselves as liars! (Verse 24.014) Were it not for the grace and mercy of Allah on you, in this world and the Hereafter, a grievous penalty would have seized you in that ye rushed glibly into this affair.

Murder

(Verse 2.178) O ye who believe! the law of equality is prescribed to you in cases of murder: the free for the free, the slave for the slave, the woman for the woman. But if any remission is made by the brother of the slain, then grant any reasonable demand, and compensate him with handsome gratitude, this is a concession and a Mercy from your Lord. After this whoever exceeds the limits shall be in grave penalty. (Verse 2.179) In the Law of Equality there is (saving of) Life to you, o ye men of understanding; that ye may restrain yourselves.

(Verse 4.092) Never should a believer kill a believer; but (If it so happens) by mistake, (Compensation is due): If one (so) kills a believer, it is ordained that he should free a believing slave, and pay compensation to the deceased's family, unless they remit it freely. If the deceased belonged to a people at war with you, and he was a believer, the freeing of a believing slave (Is enough). If he belonged to a people with whom ye have treaty of Mutual alliance, compensation should be paid to his family, and a believing slave be freed.

For those who find this beyond their means, (is prescribed) a fast for two months running: by way of repentance to Allah: for Allah hath all knowledge and all wisdom.

(Verse 4.093) If a man kills a believer intentionally, his recompense is Hell, to abide therein (For ever): And the wrath and the curse of Allah are upon him, and a dreadful penalty is prepared for him.

(Verse 5.032) On that account: We ordained for the Children of Israel that if any one slew a person - unless it be for murder or for spreading mischief in the land - it would be as if he slew the whole people: and if any one saved a life, it would be as if he saved the life of the whole people. Then although there came to them Our messengers with clear signs, yet, even after that, many of them continued to commit excesses in the land.

Theft

(Verse 5.038) As to the thief, Male or female, cut off his or her hands: a punishment by way of example, from Allah, for their crime: and Allah is Exalted in power. (Verse 5.039) But if the thief repents after his crime, and amends his conduct, Allah turneth to him in forgiveness; for Allah is Oft-forgiving, Most Merciful.

Freedom of Religion

(Verse 2.256) Let there be no compulsion in religion: Truth stands out clear from Error: whoever rejects evil and believes in Allah hath grasped the most trustworthy hand-hold, that never breaks. And Allah heareth and knoweth all things.

(Verse 2.272) It is not required of thee (O Messenger), to set them on the right path, but Allah sets on the right path whom He pleaseth. Whatever of good ye give benefits your own souls, and ye shall only do so seeking the "Face" of Allah. Whatever good ye give, shall be rendered back to you, and ye shall not Be dealt with unjustly.

(Verse 3.020) So if they dispute with thee, say: "I have submitted My whole self to Allah and so have those who follow me." And say to the People of the Book and to those who are unlearned: "Do ye (also) submit yourselves?" If they do, they are in right guidance, but if they turn back, Thy duty is to convey the Message; and in Allah's sight are (all) His servants.

(Verse 6.035) If their spurning is hard on thy mind, yet if thou wert able to seek a tunnel in the ground or a ladder to the skies and bring them a sign,- (what good?). If it were Allah's will, He could gather them together unto true guidance: so be not thou amongst those who are swayed by ignorance (and impatience)!

(Verse 6.066) But thy people reject this, though it is the truth. Say: "Not mine is the responsibility for arranging your affairs; (Verse 6.067) For every message is a limit of time, and soon shall ye know it."

(Verse 6.107) If it had been Allah's plan, they would not have taken false gods: but We made thee not one to watch over their doings, nor art thou set over them to dispose of their affairs.

(Verse 6.108) Revile not ye those whom they call upon besides Allah, lest they out of spite revile Allah in their ignorance. Thus have We made alluring to each people its own doings. In the end will they return to their Lord, and We shall then tell them the truth of all that they did.

(Verse 6.109) They swear their strongest oaths by Allah, that if a (special) sign came to them, by it they would believe. Say: "Certainly (all) signs are in the power of Allah: but what will make you (Muslims) realize that (even) if (special) signs came, they will not believe."?

(Verse 6.110) We (too) shall turn to (confusion) their hearts and their eyes, even as they refused to believe in this in the first instance: We shall leave them in their trespasses, to wander in distraction. (Verse 6.111) Even if We did send unto them angels, and the dead did speak unto them, and We gathered together all things before their very eyes, they are not the ones to believe, unless it is in Allah's plan. But most of them ignore (the truth).

(Verse 6.112) Likewise did We make for every Messenger an enemy,- evil ones among men and jinns, inspiring each other with flowery discourses by way of deception. If thy Lord had so planned, they would not have done it: so leave them and their inventions alone. (Verse 6.113) To such (deceit) let the hearts of those incline, who have no faith in the hereafter: let them delight in it, and let them earn from it what they may.

(Verse 6.125) Those whom Allah (in His plan) willeth to guide,- He openeth their breast to Islam; those whom He willeth to leave straying,- He maketh their breast close and constricted, as if they had to climb up to the skies: thus doth Allah (heap) the penalty on those who refuse to believe.

(Verse 6.137) Even so, in the eyes of most of the pagans, their "partners" made alluring the slaughter of their children, in order to lead them to their own destruction, and cause confusion in their religion. If Allah had willed, they would not have done so: But leave alone them and their inventions.

(Verse 6.149) Say: "With Allah is the argument that reaches home: if it had been His will, He could indeed have guided you all."

(Verse 10.011) If Allah were to hasten for men the ill (they have earned) as they would fain hasten on the good,- then would their respite be settled at once. But We leave those who rest not their hope on their meeting with Us, in their trespasses, wandering in distraction to and fro.

(Verse 10.099) If it had been thy Lord's will, they would all have believed,- all who are on earth! wilt thou then compel mankind, against their will, to believe! (Verse 10.100) No soul can believe, except by the will of Allah, and He will place doubt (or obscurity) on those who will not understand.

(Verse 11.008) If We delay the penalty for them for a definite term, they are sure to say, "What keeps it back?" Ah! On the day it (actually) reaches them, nothing will turn it away from them, and they will be completely encircled by that which they used to mock at! (Verse 11.009) If We give man a taste of Mercy from Ourselves, and then withdraw it from him, behold! he is in despair and (falls into) blasphemy.

(Verse 13.031) If there were a Qur'an with which mountains were moved, or the earth were cloven asunder, or the dead were made to speak, (this would be the one!) But, truly, the command is with Allah in all things! Do not the Believers know, that, had Allah (so) willed, He could have guided all mankind (to the right)? But the Unbelievers,- never will disaster cease to seize them for their (ill) deeds, or to settle close to their homes, until the promise of Allah come to pass, for, verily, Allah will not fail in His promise.

(Verse 15.003) Leave them alone, to enjoy (the good things of this life) and to please themselves: let (false) hope amuse them: soon will knowledge (undeceive them). (Verse 15.004) Never did We destroy a population that had not a term decreed and assigned beforehand.

(Verse 16.061) If Allah were to punish men for their wrong-doing, He would not leave, on the (earth), a single living creature: but He gives them respite for a stated Term: When their Term expires, they would not be able to delay (the punishment) for a single hour, just as they would not be able to anticipate it (for a single hour).

(Verse 18.029) Say, "The truth is from your Lord": Let him who will believe, and let him who will, reject (it): for the wrong-doers We have prepared a Fire whose (smoke and flames), like the walls and roof of a tent, will hem them in: if they implore relief they will be granted water like melted brass, that will scald their faces, how dreadful the drink! How uncomfortable a couch to recline on!

(Verse 18.058) But your Lord is Most forgiving, full of Mercy. If He were to call them (at once) to account for what they have earned, then surely He would have hastened their punishment: but they have their appointed time, beyond which they will find no refuge.

(Verse 22.055) Those who reject Faith will not cease to be in doubt concerning (Revelation) until the Hour (of Judgment) comes suddenly upon them, or there comes to them the Penalty of a Day of Disaster.

(Verse 26.003) It may be thou frettest thy soul with grief, that they do not become Believers. (Verse 26.004) If (such) were Our Will, We could send down to them from the sky a Sign, to which they would bend their necks in humility.

(Verse 28.055) And when they hear vain talk, they turn away therefrom and say: "To us our deeds, and to you yours; peace be to you: we seek not the ignorant." (Verse 28.056) It is true thou wilt not be able to guide every one, whom thou lovest; but Allah guides those whom He will and He knows best those who receive guidance.

(Verse 32.013) If We had so willed, We could certainly have brought every soul its true guidance: but the Word from Me will come true, "I will fill Hell with Jinns and men all together."

(Verse 35.045) If Allah were to punish men according to what they deserve. He would not leave on the back of the (earth) a single living creature: but He gives them respite for a stated Term: when their Term expires, verily Allah has in His sight all His Servants.

(Verse 43.033) And were it not that (all) men might become of one (evil) way of life, We would provide, for everyone that blasphemes against (Allah) Most Gracious, silver roofs for their houses and (silver) stair-ways on which to go up, (Verse 43.034) And (silver) doors to their houses, and thrones (of silver) on which they could recline, (Verse 43.035) And also adornments of gold. But all this were nothing but conveniences of the present life: The Hereafter, in the sight of thy Lord is for the Righteous.

(Verse 45.014) Tell those who believe, to forgive those who do not look forward to the Days of Allah: It is for Him to recompense (for good or ill) each People according to what they have earned.

133

VI

Economy, Finance & Business

Property Rights & inheritance

(Verse 2.180) It is prescribed, when death approaches any of you, if he leave any goods that he make a bequest to parents and next of kin, according to reasonable usage; this is due from the Allah- fearing. (Verse 2.181) If anyone changes the bequest after hearing it, the guilt shall be on those who make the change. For Allah hears and knows (All things).

(Verse 4.002) To orphans restore their property (When they reach their age), nor substitute (your) worthless things for (their) good ones; and devour not their substance (by mixing it up) with your own. For this is indeed a great sin.

(Verse 4.006) Make trial of orphans until they reach the age of marriage; if then ye find sound judgment in them, release their property to them; but consume it not wastefully, nor in haste against their growing up. If the guardian is well-off, Let him claim no remuneration, but if he is poor, let him have for himself what is just and reasonable. When ye release their property to them, take witnesses in their presence: But all-sufficient is Allah in taking account. (Verse 4.007) From what is left by parents and those nearest related there is a share for men and a share for women, whether the property be small or large,-a determinate share. (Verse 4.008) But if at the time of division other relatives, or orphans or poor, are present, feed them out of the (property), and speak to them words of kindness and justice. (Verse 4.009) Let those (disposing of an estate) have the same fear in their minds as they would have for their own if they had left a helpless family behind: Let them fear Allah, and speak words of appropriate (comfort).

(Verse 4.010) Those who unjustly eat up the property of orphans, eat up a

Fire into their own bodies: They will soon be enduring a Blazing Fire!

(Verse 4.011) Allah (thus) directs you as regards your Children's (Inheritance): to the male, a portion equal to that of two females: if only daughters, two or more, their share is two-thirds of the inheritance; if only one, her share is a half. For parents, a sixth share of the inheritance to each, if the deceased left children; if no children, and the parents are the (only) heirs, the mother has a third; if the deceased Left brothers (or sisters) the mother has a sixth. (The distribution in all cases ('s) after the payment of legacies and debts. Ye know not whether your parents or your children are nearest to you in benefit. These are settled portions ordained by Allah; and Allah is All-knowing, Al-wise. (Verse 4.012) In what your wives leave, your share is a half, if they leave no child; but if they leave a child, ye get a fourth; after payment of legacies and debts. In what ye leave, their share is a fourth, if ye leave no child; but if ye leave a child, they get an eighth; after payment of legacies and debts. If the man or woman whose inheritance is in question, has left neither ascendants nor descendants, but has left a brother or a sister, each one of the two gets a sixth; but if more than two, they share in a third; after payment of legacies and debts; so that no loss is caused (to any one). Thus is it ordained by Allah; and Allah is All-knowing, Most Forbearing.

(Verse 4.033) To (benefit) every one, We have appointed shares and heirs to property left by parents and relatives. To those, also, to whom your right hand was pledged, give their due portion. For truly Allah is witness to all things.

(Verse 4.176) They ask thee for a legal decision. Say: Allah directs (thus) about those who leave no descendants or ascendants as heirs. If it is a man that dies, leaving a sister but no child, she shall have half the inheritance: If (such a deceased was) a woman, who left no child, Her brother takes her inheritance: If there are two sisters, they shall have two-thirds of the inheritance (between them): if there are brothers and sisters, (they share), the male having twice the share of the female. Thus doth Allah make clear to you (His law), lest ye err. And Allah hath knowledge of all things.

(Verse 17.034) Come not nigh to the orphan's property except to improve it, until he attains the age of full strength; and fulfill (every) engagement, for (every) engagement will be enquired into (on the Day of Reckoning).

Spending & Saving

(Verse 2.188) And do not eat up your property among yourselves for vanities, nor use it as bait for the judges, with intent that ye may eat up wrongfully and knowingly a little of (other) people's property.

(Verse 2.219) They ask thee concerning wine and gambling. Say: "In them is great sin, and some profit, for men; but the sin is greater than the profit." They ask thee how much they are to spend; Say: "What is beyond your needs." Thus doth Allah Make clear to you His Signs: In order that ye may consider-

(Verse 2.254) O ye who believe! Spend out of (the bounties) We have provided for you, before the Day comes when no bargaining (Will avail), nor friendship nor intercession. Those who reject Faith they are the wrong-doers.

(Verse 3.134) Those who spend (freely), whether in prosperity, or in adversity; who restrain anger, and pardon (all) men;- for Allah loves those who do good;-

(Verse 3.180) And let not those who covetously withhold of the gifts which Allah Hath given them of His Grace, think that it is good for them: Nay, it will be the worse for them: soon shall the things which they covetously withheld be tied to their necks Like a twisted collar, on the Day of Judgment. To Allah belongs the heritage of the heavens and the earth; and Allah is well-acquainted with all that ye do.

(Verse 4.029) O ye who believe! Eat not up your property among yourselves in vanities: But let there be amongst you Traffic and trade by mutual good-will: Nor kill (or destroy) yourselves: for verily Allah hath been to you Most Merciful!

(Verse 5.087) O ye who believe! make not unlawful the good things which Allah hath made lawful for you, but commit no excess: for Allah loveth not those given to excess.

(Verse 7.031) O Children of Adam! wear your beautiful apparel at every time and place of prayer: eat and drink: But waste not by excess, for Allah loveth not the wasters.

(Verse 17.026) And render to the kindred their due rights, as (also) to those in want, and to the wayfarer: But squander not (your wealth) in the manner of a spendthrift. (Verse 17.027) Verily spendthrifts are brothers of the Evil Ones; and the Evil One is to his Lord (himself) ungrateful. (Verse 17.028) And even if thou hast to turn away from them in pursuit of the Mercy from thy Lord which thou dost expect, yet speak to them a word of easy kindness. (Verse 17.029) Make not thy hand tied (like a niggard's) to thy neck, nor stretch it forth to its utmost reach, so that thou become blameworthy and destitute.

(Verse 25.067) Those who, when they spend, are not extravagant and not niggardly, but hold a just (balance) between those (extremes);

Interest & Lending

(Verse 2.275) Those who devour usury will not stand except as stand one whom the Evil one by his touch Hath driven to madness. That is because they say: "Trade is like usury," but Allah hath permitted trade and forbidden usury. Those who after receiving direction from their Lord, desist, shall be pardoned for the past; their case is for Allah (to judge); but those who repeat (The offence) are companions of the Fire: They will abide therein (for ever). (Verse 2.276) Allah will deprive usury of all blessing, but will give increase for deeds of charity: For He loveth not creatures ungrateful and wicked.

(Verse 2.278) O ye who believe! Fear Allah, and give up what remains of your demand for usury, if ye are indeed believers. (Verse 2.279) If ye do it not, Take notice of war from Allah and His Messenger: But if ye turn back, ye shall have your capital sums: Deal not unjustly, and ye shall not be dealt with unjustly. (Verse 2.280) If the debtor is in a difficulty, grant him time Till it is easy for him to repay. But if ye remit it by way of charity, that is best for you if ye only knew.

(Verse 3.130) O ye who believe! Devour not usury, doubled and multiplied; but fear Allah; that ye may (really) prosper.

(Verse 4.161) That they took usury, though they were forbidden; and that they devoured men's substance wrongfully;- we have prepared for those among them who reject faith a grievous punishment.

Transaction & Contracts

(Verse 2.282) O ye who believe! When ye deal with each other, in transactions involving future obligations in a fixed period of time, reduce them to writing Let a scribe write down faithfully as between the parties: let not the scribe refuse to write: as Allah Has taught him, so let him write. Let him who incurs the liability dictate, but let him fear His Lord Allah, and not diminish aught of what he owes. If they party liable is mentally deficient, or weak, or unable Himself to dictate, Let his guardian dictate faithfully, and get two witnesses, out of your own men, and if there are not two men, then a man and two women, such as ye choose, for witnesses, so that if one of them errs, the other can remind her. The witnesses should not refuse when they are called on (For evidence). Disdain not to reduce to writing (your contract) for a future period, whether it be small or big: it is juster in the sight of Allah, More suitable as evidence, and more convenient to prevent doubts among yourselves but if it be a transaction which ye carry out on the spot among yourselves, there is no blame on you if ye reduce it not to writing. But take witness whenever ye make a commercial contract; and let neither scribe nor witness suffer harm. If ye do (such harm), it would be wickedness in you. So fear Allah; For it is Good that teaches you. And Allah is well acquainted with all things. If ye are on a journey, and cannot find a scribe, a pledge with possession (may serve the purpose). And if one of you deposits a thing on trust with another, let the trustee (faithfully) discharge his trust, and let him Fear his Lord conceal not evidence; for whoever conceals it, - his heart is tainted with sin. And Allah knoweth all that ye do.

(Verse 2.283) If ye are on a journey, and cannot find a scribe, a pledge with possession (may serve the purpose). And if one of you deposits a thing on trust with another, Let the trustee (Faithfully) discharge His trust, and let him fear his Lord. Conceal not evidence; for whoever conceals it,- His heart is tainted with sin. And Allah Knoweth all that ye do.

(Verse 7.085) To the Madyan people We sent Shu'aib, one of their own brethren: he said: "O my people! worship Allah; Ye have no other god but Him. Now hath come unto you a clear (Sign) from your Lord! Give just measure and weight, nor withhold from the people the things that are their due; and do no mischief on the earth after it has been set in order: that will be best for you, if ye have Faith.

(Verse 8.027) O ye that believe! betray not the trust of Allah and the Messenger, nor misappropriate knowingly things entrusted to you.

(Verse 11.084) To the Madyan People (We sent) Shu'aib, one of their own brethren: he said: "O my people! worship Allah: Ye have no other god but Him. And give not short measure or weight: I see you in prosperity, but I fear for you the penalty of a day that will compass (you) all round. (Verse 11.085) "And O my people! give just measure and weight, nor withhold from the people the things that are their due: commit not evil in the land with intent to do mischief. (Verse 11.086) "That which is left you by Allah is best for you, if ye (but) believed! but I am not set over you to keep watch!"

(Verse 17.035) Give full measure when ye measure, and weigh with a balance that is straight: that is the most fitting and the most advantageous in the final determination.

(Verse 26.181) "Give just measure, and cause no loss (to others by fraud). (Verse 26.182) "And weigh with scales true and upright. (Verse 26.183) "And withhold not things justly due to men, nor do evil in the land, working mischief.

(Verse 55.009) So establish weight with justice and fall not short in the balance.

(Verse 83.001) Woe to those that deal in fraud,- (Verse 83.002) Those who, when they have to receive by measure from men, exact full measure, (Verse 83.003) But when they have to give by measure or weight to men, give less than due.

Wealth

(Verse 2.188) And do not eat up your property among yourselves for vanities, nor use it as bait for the judges, with intent that ye may eat up wrongfully and knowingly a little of (other) people's property.

(Verse 3.014) Fair in the eyes of men is the love of things they covet: Women and sons; Heaped-up hoards of gold and silver; horses branded (for blood and excellence); and (wealth of) cattle and well-tilled land. Such are the possessions of this world's life; but in nearness to Allah is the best of the goals (To return to).

(Verse 3.180) And let not those who covetously withhold of the gifts which Allah Hath given them of His Grace, think that it is good for them: Nay, it will be the worse for them: soon shall the things which they covetously withheld be tied to their necks Like a twisted collar, on the Day of Judgment. To Allah belongs the heritage of the heavens and the earth; and Allah is well-acquainted with all that ye do. (Verse 3.181) Allah hath heard the taunt of those who say: "Truly, Allah is indigent and we are rich!"- We shall certainly record their word and (their act) of slaying the prophets in defiance of right, and We shall say: "Taste ye the penalty of the Scorching Fire!

(Verse 4.037) (Nor) those who are niggardly or enjoin niggardliness on others, or hide the bounties which Allah hath bestowed on them; for We have prepared, for those who resist Faith, a punishment that steeps them in contempt;- (Verse 4.038) Not those who spend of their substance, to be seen of men, but have no faith in Allah and the Last Day: If any take the Evil One for their intimate, what a dreadful intimate he is! (Verse 4.039) And what burden Were it on them if they had faith in Allah and in the Last Day, and they spent out of what Allah hath given them for sustenance? For Allah hath full knowledge of them.

(Verse 8.028) And know ye that your possessions and your progeny are but a trial; and that it is Allah with Whom lies your highest reward.

(Verse 16.071) Allah has bestowed His gifts of sustenance more freely on some of you than on others: those more favored are not going to throw back their gifts to those whom their right hands possess, so as to be equal in that respect. Will they then deny the favors of Allah?

(Verse 16.075) Allah sets forth the Parable (of two men: one) a slave under the dominion of another; He has no power of any sort; and (the other) a man on whom We have bestowed goodly favors from Ourselves, and he spends thereof (freely), privately and publicly: are the two equal? (By no means;) praise be to Allah. But most of them understand not.

(Verse 17.020) Of the bounties of thy Lord We bestow freely on all- These as well as those: The bounties of thy Lord are not closed (to anyone). (Verse 17.021) See how We have bestowed more on some than on others; but verily the Hereafter is more in rank and gradation and more in excellence.

(Verse 17.030) Verily thy Lord doth provide sustenance in abundance for whom He pleaseth, and He provideth in a just measure. For He doth know and regard all His servants.

(Verse 20.131) Nor strain thine eyes in longing for the things We have given for enjoyment to parties of them, the splendor of the life of this world, through which We test them: but the provision of thy Lord is better and more enduring.

(Verse 21.013) Flee not, but return to the good things of this life which were given you, and to your homes in order that ye may be called to account.

(Verse 24.022) Let not those among you who are endued with grace and amplitude of means resolve by oath against helping their kinsmen, those in want, and those who have left their homes in Allah's cause: let them forgive and overlook, do you not wish that Allah should forgive you? For Allah is Oft-Forgiving, Most Merciful.

(Verse 28.060) The (material) things which ye are given are but the conveniences of this life and the glitter thereof; but that which is with Allah is better and more enduring: will ye not then be wise? (Verse 28.061) Are (these two) alike?- one to whom We have made a goodly promise, and who is going to reach its (fulfillment), and one to whom We have given the good things of this life, but who, on the Day of Judgment, is to be among those brought up (for punishment)?

(Verse 28.078) He said: "This has been given to me because of a certain knowledge which I have." Did he not know that Allah had destroyed, before him, (whole) generations,- which were superior to him in strength and greater in the amount (of riches) they had collected? but the wicked are not called (immediately) to account for their sins. (Verse 28.079) So he went forth among his people in the (pride of his worldly) glitter. Said those whose aim is the Life of this World: "Oh! that we had the like of what Quran has got! for he is truly a lord of mighty good fortune!" (Verse 28.080) But those who had been granted (true) knowledge said: "Alas for you! The reward of Allah (in the Hereafter) is best for those who believe and work righteousness: but this none shall attain, save those who steadfastly persevere (in good)." (Verse 28.081) Then We caused the earth to swallow up him and his house; and he had not (the least little) party to help him against Allah, nor could he defend himself. (Verse 28.082) And those who had envied his position the day before began to say on the morrow: "Ah! it is indeed Allah Who enlarges the provision or restricts it, to any of His servants He pleases! had it not been that Allah was gracious to us, He could have caused the earth to swallow us up! Ah! those who reject Allah will assuredly never prosper."

(Verse 29.062) Allah enlarges the sustenance (which He gives) to whichever of His servants He pleases; and He (similarly) grants by (strict) measure, (as He pleases): for Allah has full knowledge of all things.

(Verse 30.037) See they not that Allah enlarges the provision and restricts it, to whomsoever He pleases? Verily in that are Signs for those who believe.

(Verse 34.034) Never did We send a Warner to a population, but the wealthy ones among them said: "We believe not in the (Message) with which ye have been sent." (Verse 34.035) They said: "We have more in wealth and in sons, and we cannot be punished." (Verse 34.036) Say: "Verily my Lord enlarges and restricts the Provision to whom He pleases, but most men understand not." (Verse 34.037) It is not your wealth nor your sons, that will bring you nearer to Us in degree: but only those who believe and work righteousness - these are the ones for whom there is a multiplied Reward for their deeds, while secure they (reside) in the dwellings on high!

(Verse 34.039) Say: "Verily my Lord enlarges and restricts the Sustenance to such of his servants as He pleases: and nothing do ye spend in the least (in His cause) but He replaces it: for He is the Best of those who grant Sustenance.

(Verse 35.002) What Allah out of his Mercy doth bestow on mankind there is none can withhold: what He doth withhold, there is none can grant, apart from Him: and He is the Exalted in Power, full of Wisdom.

(Verse 36.047) And when they are told, "Spend ye of (the bounties) with which Allah has provided you," the Unbelievers say to those who believe: "Shall we then feed those whom, if Allah had so willed, He would have fed, (Himself)?- Ye are in nothing but manifest error."

(Verse 39.052) Know they not that Allah enlarges the provision or restricts it, for any He pleases? Verily, in this are Signs for those who believe!

(Verse 42.012) To Him belong the keys of the heavens and the earth: He enlarges and restricts. The Sustenance to whom He will: for He knows full well all things.

(Verse 42.027) If Allah were to enlarge the provision for His Servants, they would indeed transgress beyond all bounds through the earth; but he sends (it) down in due measure as He pleases. For He is with His Servants Well-acquainted, Watchful.

(Verse 43.032) Is it they who would portion out the Mercy of thy Lord? It is We Who portion out between them their livelihood in the life of this world: and We raise some of them above others in ranks, so that some may command work from others. But the Mercy of thy Lord is better than the (wealth) which they amass.

(Verse 51.019) And in their wealth and possessions (was remembered) the right of the (needy,) him who asked, and him who (for some reason) was prevented (from asking).

(Verse 63.009) O ye who believe! Let not your riches or your children divert you from the remembrance of Allah. If any act thus, the loss is their own. (Verse 63.010) and spend something (in charity) out of the substance which We have bestowed on you, before Death should come to any of you and he should say, "O my Lord! why didst Thou not give me respite for a little while? I should then have given (largely) in charity, and I should have been one of the doers of good".

(Verse 64.015) Your riches and your children may be but a trial: but in the Presence of Allah, is the highest, Reward.

(Verse 70.018) And collect (wealth) and hide it (from use)!

(Verse 70.024) And those in whose wealth is a recognized right. (Verse 70.025) For the (needy) who asks and him who is prevented (for some reason from asking);

(Verse 71.021) Noah said: "O my Lord! They have disobeyed me, but they follow (men) whose wealth and children give them no increase but only Loss.

(Verse 74.011) Leave Me alone, (to deal) with the (creature) whom I created (bare and) alone!- (Verse 74.012) To whom I granted resources in abundance, (Verse 74.013) And sons to be by his side!- (Verse 74.014) To whom I made (life) smooth and comfortable! (Verse 74.015) Yet is he greedy-that I should add (yet more);- (Verse 74.016) By no means! For to Our Signs he has been refractory!

(Verse 89.015) Now, as for man, when his Lord trieth him, giving him honor and gifts, then saith he, (puffed up), "My Lord hath honored me." (Verse 89.016) But when He trieth him, restricting his subsistence for him, then saith he (in despair), "My Lord hath humiliated me!" (Verse 89.017) Nay, nay! but ye honour not the orphans! (Verse 89.018) Nor do ye encourage one another to feed the poor!- (Verse 89.019) And ye devour inheritance - all with greed, (Verse 89.020) And ye love wealth with inordinate love!

(Verse 100.008) And violent is he in his love of wealth.

(Verse 102.001) The mutual rivalry for piling up (the good things

of this world) diverts you (from the more serious things), (Verse 104.002) Who pileth up wealth and layeth it by, (Verse 104.003) Thinking that his wealth would make him last for ever! (Verse 111.002) No profit to him from all his wealth, and all his gains!

VII

State Relations & Security

State Security

(Verse 2.190) Fight in the cause of Allah those who fight you, but do not transgress limits; for Allah loveth not transgressors. (Verse 2.191) And slay them wherever ye catch them, and turn them out from where they have Turned you out; for tumult and oppression are worse than slaughter; but fight them not at the Sacred Mosque, unless they (first) fight you there; but if they fight you, slay them. Such is the reward of those who suppress faith. (Verse 2.192) But if they cease, Allah is Oft-forgiving, Most Merciful. (Verse 2.193) And fight them on until there is no more tumult or oppression, and there prevail justice and faith in Allah; but if they cease, Let there be no hostility except to those who practice oppression.

(Verse 2.216) Fighting is prescribed for you, and ye dislike it. But it is possible that ye dislike a thing which is good for you, and that ye love a thing which is bad for you. But Allah knoweth, and ye know not. (Verse 2.217) They ask thee concerning fighting in the Prohibited Month. Say: "Fighting therein is a grave (offence); but graver is it in the sight of Allah to prevent access to the path of Allah, to deny Him, to prevent access to the Sacred Mosque, and drive out its members." Tumult and oppression are worse than slaughter. Nor will they cease fighting you until they turn you back from your faith if they can. And if any of you Turn back from their faith and die in unbelief, their works will bear no fruit in this life and in the Hereafter; they will be companions of the Fire and will abide therein.

(Verse 2.244) Then fight in the cause of Allah, and know that Allah Heareth and knoweth all things.

(Verse 3.013) "There has already been for you a Sign in the two armies that met (in combat): One was fighting in the cause of Allah, the other resisting Allah; these saw with their own eyes twice their number. But Allah doth support with His aid whom He pleaseth. In this is a warning for such as have eyes to see."

(Verse 3.146) How many of the prophets fought (in Allah's way), and with them (fought) Large bands of godly men? But they never lost heart if they met with disaster in Allah's way, nor did they weaken (in will) nor give in. And Allah Loves those who are firm and steadfast.

(Verse 4.075) And why should ye not fight in the cause of Allah and of those who, being weak, are ill-treated (and oppressed)?- Men, women, and children, whose cry is: "Our Lord! Rescue us from this town, whose people are oppressors; and raise for us from thee one who will protect; and raise for us from thee one who will help!" (Verse 4.076) Those who believe fight in the cause of Allah, and those who reject Faith Fight in the cause of Evil: So fight ye against the friends of Satan: feeble indeed is the cunning of Satan. (Verse 4.077) Hast thou not turned Thy vision to those who were told to hold back their hands (from fight) but establish regular prayers and spend in regular charity? When (at length) the order for fighting was issued to them, behold! a section of them feared men as - or even more than - they should have feared Allah: They said: "Our Lord! Why hast Thou ordered us to fight? Wouldst Thou not Grant us respite to our (natural) term, near (enough)?" Say: "Short is the enjoyment of this world: the Hereafter is the best for those who do right: Never will ye be dealt with unjustly in the very least!

(Verse 4.089) They but wish that ye should reject Faith, as they do, and thus be on the same footing (as they): But take not friends from their ranks until they flee in the way of Allah (From what is forbidden). But if they turn renegades, seize them and slay them wherever ye find them; and (in any case) take no friends or helpers from their ranks;- (Verse 4.090) Except those who join a group between whom and you there is a treaty (of peace), or those who approach you with hearts restraining them from fighting you as well as fighting their own people. If Allah had pleased, He could have given them power over you, and they would have fought you: Therefore if they withdraw from you but fight you not, and (instead) send you (Guarantees of) peace, then Allah Hath opened no way for you (to war against them).

(Verse 4.091) Others you will find that wish to gain your confidence as well as that of their people: Every time they are sent back to temptation, they succumb thereto: if they withdraw not from you nor give you (guarantees) of peace besides restraining their hands, seize them and slay them wherever ye get them: In their case We have provided you with a clear argument against them. (Verse 4.092) Never should a believer kill a believer; but (If it so happens) by mistake, (Compensation is due): If one (so) kills a believer, it is ordained that he should free a believing slave, and pay compensation to the deceased's family, unless they remit it freely. If the deceased belonged to a people at war with you, and he was a believer, the freeing of a believing slave (Is enough). If he belonged to a people with whom ye have treaty of Mutual alliance, compensation should be paid to his family, and a believing slave be freed. For those who find this beyond their means, (is prescribed) a fast for two months running: by way of repentance to Allah: for Allah hath all knowledge and all wisdom.

(Verse 4.104) And slacken not in following up the enemy: If ye are suffering hardships, they are suffering similar hardships; but ye have Hope from Allah, while they have none. And Allah is full of knowledge and wisdom.

(Verse 5.033) The punishment of those who wage war against Allah and His Messenger, and strive with might and main for mischief through the land is: execution, or crucifixion, or the cutting off of hands and feet from opposite sides, or exile from the land: that is their disgrace in this world, and a heavy punishment is theirs in the Hereafter; (Verse 5.034) Except for those who repent before they fall into your power: in that case, know that Allah is Oft-forgiving, Most Merciful.

(Verse 5.035) O ye who believe! Do your duty to Allah, seek the means of approach unto Him, and strive with might and main in his cause: that ye may prosper.

(Verse 8.015) O ye who believe! when ye meet the Unbelievers in hostile array, never turn your backs to them. (Verse 8.016) If any do turn his back to them on such a day - unless it be in a stratagem of war, or to retreat to a troop (of his own)- he draws on himself the wrath of Allah, and his abode is

Hell,- an evil refuge (indeed)!

(Verse 8.039) And fight them on until there is no more tumult or oppression, and there prevail justice and faith in Allah altogether and everywhere; but if they cease, verily Allah doth see all that they do.

(Verse 8.045) O ye who believe! When ye meet a force, be firm, and call Allah in remembrance much (and often); that ye may prosper:

(Verse 8.057) If ye gain the mastery over them in war, disperse, with them, those who follow them, that they may remember. (Verse 8.058) If thou fearest treachery from any group, throw back (their covenant) to them, (so as to be) on equal terms: for Allah loveth not the treacherous. (Verse 8.059) Let not the unbelievers think that they can get the better (of the godly): they will never frustrate (them). (Verse 8.060) Against them make ready your strength to the utmost of your power, including steeds of war, to strike terror into (the hearts of) the enemies, of Allah and your enemies, and others besides, whom ye may not know, but whom Allah doth know. Whatever ye shall spend in the cause of Allah, shall be repaid unto you, and ye shall not be treated unjustly. (Verse 8.061) But if the enemy incline towards peace, do thou (also) incline towards peace, and trust in Allah: for He is One that heareth and knoweth (all things). (Verse 8.062) Should they intend to deceive thee,- verily Allah sufficeth thee: He it is That hath strengthened thee with His aid and with (the company of) the Believers;

(Verse 8.065) O Prophet! Rouse the Believers to the fight. If there are twenty amongst you, patient and persevering, they will vanquish two hundred: if a hundred, they will vanquish a thousand of the Unbelievers: for these are a people without understanding.

(Verse 8.066) For the present, Allah hath lightened your (task), for He knoweth that there is a weak spot in you: But (even so), if there are a hundred of you, patient and persevering, they will vanquish two hundred, and if a thousand, they will vanquish two thousand, with the leave of Allah: for Allah is with those who patiently persevere. (Verse 8.067) It is not fitting for a prophet that he should have prisoners of war until he hath thoroughly subdued the land. Ye look for the temporal goods of this world; but Allah looketh to the Hereafter: And Allah is Exalted in might, Wise.

(Verse 9.029) Fight those who believe not in Allah nor the Last Day, nor hold that forbidden which hath been forbidden by Allah and His Messenger, nor acknowledge the religion of Truth, (even if they are) of the People of the Book, until they pay the Jizya with willing submission, and feel themselves subdued.

(Verse 9.088) But the Messenger, and those who believe with him, strive and fight with their wealth and their persons: for them are (all) good things: and it is they who will prosper.

(Verse 9.090) And there were, among the desert Arabs (also), men who made excuses and came to claim exemption; and those who were false to Allah and His Messenger (merely) sat inactive. Soon will a grievous penalty seize the Unbelievers among them. (Verse 9.091) There is no blame on those who are infirm, or ill, or who find no resources to spend (on the cause), if they are sincere (in duty) to Allah and His Messenger: no ground (of complaint) can there be against such as do right: and Allah is Oft-forgiving, Most Merciful. (Verse 9.092) Nor (is there blame) on those who came to thee to be provided with mounts, and when thou saidst, "I can find no mounts for you," they turned back, their eyes streaming with tears of grief that they had no resources wherewith to provide the expenses.

(Verse 9.111) Allah hath purchased of the believers their persons and their goods; for theirs (in return) is the garden (of Paradise): they fight in His cause, and slay and are slain: a promise binding on Him in truth, through the Law, the Gospel, and the Qur'an: and who is more faithful to his covenant than Allah? then rejoice in the bargain which ye have concluded: that is the achievement supreme.

(Verse 9.122) Nor should the Believers all go forth together: if a contingent from every expedition remained behind, they could devote themselves to studies in religion, and admonish the people when they return to them,- that thus they (may learn) to guard themselves (against evil). (Verse 9.123) O ye who believe! fight the unbelievers who gird you about, and let them find firmness in you: and know that Allah is with those who fear Him.

(Verse 22.039) To those against whom war is made, permission is given (to fight), because they are wronged;- and verily, Allah is most powerful for their aid;- (Verse 22.040) (They are) those who have been expelled from their homes in defiance of right,- (for no cause) except that they say, "our Lord is Allah". Did not Allah check one set of people by means of another, there would surely have been pulled down monasteries, churches, synagogues, and mosques, in which the name of Allah is commemorated in abundant measure. Allah will certainly aid those who aid his (cause);- for verily Allah is full of Strength, Exalted in Might, (able to enforce His Will).

(Verse 42.039) And those who, when an oppressive wrong is inflicted on them, (are not cowed but) help and defend themselves.

(Verse 47.004) Therefore, when ye meet the Unbelievers (in fight), smite at their necks; At length, when ye have thoroughly subdued them, bind a bond firmly (on them): thereafter (is the time for) either generosity or ransom: Until the war lays down its burdens. Thus (are ye commanded): but if it had been Allah's Will, He could certainly have exacted retribution from them (Himself); but (He lets you fight) in order to test you, some with others. But those who are slain in the Way of Allah,- He will never let their deeds be lost.

(Verse 60.008) Allah forbids you not, with regard to those who fight you not for (your) Faith nor drive you out of your homes, from dealing kindly and justly with them: for Allah loveth those who are just. (Verse 60.009) Allah only forbids you, with regard to those who fight you for (your) Faith, and drive you out of your homes, and support (others) in driving you out, from turning to them (for friendship and protection). It is such as turn to them (in these circumstances), that do wrong.

Soldiers & Martyrs

(Verse 3.139) So lose not heart, nor fall into despair: For ye must gain mastery if ye are true in Faith. (Verse 3.140) If a wound hath touched you, be sure a similar wound hath touched the others. Such days (of varying fortunes) We give to men and men by turns: that Allah may know those that believe, and that He may take to Himself from your ranks Martyr-witnesses (to Truth). And Allah loveth not those that do wrong. (Verse 3.141) Allah's object also is to purge those that are true in Faith and to deprive of blessing Those that resist Faith. (Verse 3.142) Did ye think that ye would enter Heaven without Allah testing those of you who fought hard (In His Cause) and remained steadfast?

(Verse 3.169) Think not of those who are slain in Allah's way as dead. Nay, they live, finding their sustenance in the presence of their Lord; (Verse 3.170) They rejoice in the bounty provided by Allah: And with regard to those left behind, who have not yet joined them (in their bliss), the (Martyrs) glory in the fact that on them is no fear, nor have they (cause to) grieve.

(Verse 3.195) And their Lord hath accepted of them, and answered them: "Never will I suffer to be lost the work of any of you, be he male or female: Ye are members, one of another: Those who have left their homes, or been driven out therefrom, or suffered harm in My Cause, or fought or been slain,- verily, I will blot out from them their iniquities, and admit them into Gardens with rivers flowing beneath;- A reward from the presence of Allah, and from His presence is the best of rewards."

(Verse 4.095) Not equal are those believers who sit (at home) and receive no hurt, and those who strive and fight in the cause of Allah with their goods and their persons. Allah hath granted a grade higher to those who strive and fight with their goods and persons than to those who sit (at home). Unto all (in Faith) Hath Allah promised good: But those who strive and fight Hath He distinguished above those who sit (at home) by a special reward,- (Verse 4.096) Ranks specially bestowed by Him, and Forgiveness and Mercy. For Allah is Oft-forgiving, Most Merciful.

(Verse 4.100) He who forsakes his home in the cause of Allah, finds in the earth Many a refuge, wide and spacious: Should he die as a refugee from home for Allah and His Messenger, His reward becomes due and sure with Allah: And Allah is Oft- forgiving, Most Merciful.

(Verse 8.074) Those who believe, and adopt exile, and fight for the Faith, in the cause of Allah as well as those who give (them) asylum and aid,- these are (all) in very truth the Believers: for them is the forgiveness of sins and a provision most generous. (Verse 8.075) And those who accept Faith subsequently, and adopt exile, and fight for the Faith in your company,- they are of you. But kindred by blood have prior rights against each other in the Book of Allah. Verily Allah is well-acquainted with all things.

(Verse 9.020) Those who believe, and suffer exile and strive with might and main, in Allah's cause, with their goods and their persons, have the highest rank in the sight of Allah: they are the people who will achieve (salvation).

(Verse 9.041) Go ye forth, (whether equipped) lightly or heavily, and strive and struggle, with your goods and your persons, in the cause of Allah. That is best for you, if ye (but) knew. (Verse 9.042) If there had been immediate gain (in sight), and the journey easy, they would (all) without doubt have followed thee, but the distance was long, (and weighed) on them. They would indeed swear by Allah, "If we only could, we should certainly have come out with you": They would destroy their own souls; for Allah doth know that they are certainly lying. (Verse 9.043) Allah give thee grace! why didst thou grant them until those who told the truth were seen by thee in a clear light, and thou hadst proved the liars? (Verse 9.044) Those who believe in Allah and the Last Day ask thee for no exemption from fighting with their goods and persons. And Allah knoweth well those who do their duty. (Verse 9.045) Only those ask thee for exemption who believe not in Allah and the Last Day, and whose hearts are in doubt, so that they are tossed in their doubts to and fro.

(Verse 9.046) If they had intended to come out, they would certainly have made some preparation therefor; but Allah was averse to their being sent forth; so He made them lag behind, and they were told, "Sit ye among those who sit (inactive)." (Verse 9.047) If they had come out with you, they would not have added to your (strength) but only (made for) disorder, hurrying to and fro in your midst and sowing sedition among you, and there would have been some among you who would have listened to them. But Allah knoweth well those who do wrong.

(Verse 9.052) Say: "Can you expect for us (any fate) other than one of two glorious things- (Martyrdom or victory)? But we can expect for you either that Allah will send his punishment from Himself, or by our hands. So wait (expectant); we too will wait with you."

(Verse 9.100) The vanguard (of Islam)- the first of those who forsook (their homes) and of those who gave them aid, and (also) those who follow them in (all) good deeds,- well-pleased is Allah with them, as are they with Him: for them hath He prepared gardens under which rivers flow, to dwell therein for ever: that is the supreme felicity.

(Verse 16.041) To those who leave their homes in the cause of Allah, after suffering oppression,- We will assuredly give a goodly home in this world; but truly the reward of the Hereafter will be greater. If they only realized (this)!

(Verse 16.110) But verily thy Lord,- to those who leave their homes after trials and persecutions,- and who thereafter strive and fight for the faith and patiently persevere,- Thy Lord, after all this is oft-forgiving, Most Merciful.

(Verse 22.058) Those who leave their homes in the cause of Allah, and are then slain or die,- On them will Allah bestow verily a goodly Provision: Truly Allah is He Who bestows the best provision.

(Verse 24.053) They swear their strongest oaths by Allah that, if only thou wouldst command them, they would leave (their homes). Say: "Swear ye not; Obedience is (more) reasonable; verily, Allah is well acquainted with all that ye do."

(Verse 29.002) Do men think that they will be left alone on saying, "We believe", and that they will not be tested?

(Verse 33.013) Behold! A party among them said: "Ye men of Yathrib! ye cannot stand (the attack)! therefore go back!" And a band of them ask for leave of the Prophet, saying, "Truly our houses are bare and exposed," though they were not exposed they intended nothing but to run away.

(Verse 33.018) Verily Allah knows those among you who keep back (men) and those who say to their brethren, "Come along to us", but come not to the fight except for just a little while.

(Verse 48.017) No blame is there on the blind, nor is there blame on the lame, nor on one ill (if he joins not the war): But he that obeys Allah and his Messenger,- (Allah) will admit him to Gardens beneath which rivers flow; and he who turns back, (Allah) will punish him with a grievous Penalty.

(Verse 61.004) Truly Allah loves those who fight in His Cause in battle array, as if they were a solid cemented structure.

(Verse 61.011) That ye believe in Allah and His Messenger, and that ye strive (your utmost) in the Cause of Allah, with your property and your persons: That will be best for you, if ye but knew!

State Relations

(Verse 2.251) By Allah's will they routed them; and David slew Goliath; and Allah gave him power and wisdom and taught him whatever (else) He willed. And did not Allah check one set of people by means of another, the earth would indeed be full of mischief: But Allah is full of bounty to all the worlds.

(Verse 2.253) Those messengers We endowed with gifts, some above others: To one of them Allah spoke; others He raised to degrees (of honor); to Jesus the son of Mary We gave clear (Signs), and strengthened him with the holy spirit. If Allah had so willed, succeeding generations would not have fought among each other, after clear (Signs) had come to them, but they (chose) to wrangle, some believing and others rejecting. If Allah had so willed, they would not have fought each other; but Allah Fulfilleth His plan.

(Verse 3.028) Let not the believers take for friends or helpers Unbelievers rather than believers: if any do that, in nothing will there be help from Allah: except by way of precaution, that ye may Guard yourselves from them. But Allah cautions you (To remember) Himself; for the final goal is to Allah.

(Verse 3.118) O ye who believe! Take not into your intimacy those outside your ranks: They will not fail to corrupt you. They only desire your ruin: Rank hatred has already appeared from their mouths: What their hearts conceal is far worse. We have made plain to you the Signs, if ye have wisdom.

(Verse 4.094) O ye who believe! When ye go abroad in the cause of Allah, investigate carefully, and say not to any one who offers you a salutation: "Thou art none of a believer!" Coveting the perishable goods of this life: with Allah are profits and spoils abundant. Even thus were ye yourselves before, till Allah conferred on you His favors: Therefore carefully investigate. For

Allah is well aware of all that ye do.

(Verse 4.139) Yea, to those who take for friends unbelievers rather than believers: is it honor they seek among them? Nay,- all honor is with Allah.

(Verse 5.051) O ye who believe! take not the Jews and the Christians for your friends and protectors: They are but friends and protectors to each other. And he amongst you that turns to them (for friendship) is of them. Verily Allah guideth not a people unjust.

(Verse 5.055) Your (real) friends are (no less than) Allah, His Messenger, and the (fellowship of) believers,- those who establish regular prayers and regular charity, and they bow down humbly (in worship).

(Verse 5.057) O ye who believe! take not for friends and protectors those who take your religion for a mockery or sport,- whether among those who received the Scripture before you, or among those who reject Faith; but fear ye Allah, if ye have faith (indeed).

(Verse 5.082) Strongest among men in enmity to the believers wilt thou find the Jews and Pagans; and nearest among them in love to the believers wilt thou find those who say, "We are Christians": because amongst these are men devoted to learning and men who have renounced the world, and they are not arrogant.

(Verse 8.058) If thou fearest treachery from any group, throw back (their covenant) to them, (so as to be) on equal terms: for Allah loveth not the treacherous. (Verse 8.059) Let not the unbelievers think that they can get the better (of the godly): they will never frustrate (them). (Verse 8.060) Against them make ready your strength to the utmost of your power, including steeds of war, to strike terror into (the hearts of) the enemies, of Allah and your enemies, and others besides, whom ye may not know, but whom Allah doth know. Whatever ye shall spend in the cause of Allah, shall be repaid unto you, and ye shall not be treated unjustly.

(Verse 8.072) Those who believed, and adopted exile, and fought for the Faith, with their property and their persons, in the cause of Allah, as well as those who gave (them) asylum and aid,- these are (all) friends and protectors, one of another. As to those who believed but came not into exile, ye owe no duty of protection to them until they come into exile; but if they seek your aid in religion, it is your duty to help them, except against a people with whom ye have a treaty of mutual alliance. And (remember) Allah seeth all that ye do. (Verse 8.073) The Unbelievers are protectors, one of another: Unless ye do this, (protect each other), there would be tumult and oppression on earth, and great mischief.

(Verse 9.004) (But the treaties are) not dissolved with those Pagans with whom ye have entered into alliance and who have not subsequently failed you in aught, nor aided any one against you. So fulfill your engagements with them to the end of their term: for Allah loveth the righteous.

(Verse 29.046) And dispute ye not with the People of the Book, except with means better (than mere disputation), unless it be with those of them who inflict wrong (and injury): but say, "We believe in the revelation which has come down to us and in that which came down to you; Our Allah and your Allah is one; and it is to Him we bow (in Islam)."

(Verse 49.010) The Believers are but a single Brotherhood: So make peace and reconciliation between your two (contending) brothers; and fear Allah, that ye may receive Mercy.

(Verse 60.001) O ye who believe! Take not my enemies and yours as friends (or protectors),- offering them (your) love, even though they have rejected the Truth that has come to you, and have (on the contrary) driven out the Prophet and yourselves (from your homes), (simply) because ye believe in Allah your Lord! If ye have come out to strive in My Way and to seek My Good Pleasure, (take them not as friends), holding secret converse of love (and friendship) with them: for I know full well all that ye conceal and all that ye reveal. And any of you that does this has strayed from the Straight Path.

(Verse 60.002) If they were to get the better of you, they would behave to you as enemies, and stretch forth their hands and their tongues against you for evil: and they desire that ye should reject the Truth.

(Verse 60.013) O ye who believe! Turn not (for friendship) to people on whom is the Wrath of Allah, of the Hereafter they are already in despair, just as the Unbelievers are in despair about those (buried) in graves.

About the Author

Abdul Quayyum Khan Kundi is known for his contributions to Pakistani newspapers through op-ed columns. He has shared his insights on a wide range of topics including politics, social issues, and foreign policy. His writing has appeared in prominent publications such as Independent Urdu, The Daily Times, The Frontier Post, and Pakistan Today.

In a particular op-ed column dated December 14, 2011, Mr. Kundi discussed the emergence of a new multi-polar world order. He argued that American hegemony was being challenged by a collaborative effort between China and Russia, leading to the development of a new cold war scenario. This topic reflects his engagement with global geopolitics and international relations.

Mr. Kundi has also authored several books that delve into various subjects. His first book, "Freedom by Choice," is a compilation of writings that explore US-Pakistan relations, reforms in the Muslim world, and the balance of power in South Asia. This book showcases his keen interest in diplomacy and regional dynamics.

"Lessons from the Quran," his second book, focuses on Quranic verses with an emphasis on their relevance to social values. This work highlights his engagement with religious and ethical matters.

His book titled "Islamic Social Contract" is a significant effort to propose a political system rooted in the social values outlined in the Quran and the Sunnah (tradition) of the Prophet Mohammad (PBUH). Mr. Kundi believes that the Muslim world's political liberation can only be achieved by developing systems that align with Islamic cultural traditions. This book offers a framework for building stable societies, drawing from the context of reform movements like the "Arab Spring."

Finally, his book "Thoughts" is a collection of metaphysical speculations covering topics related to religion, philosophy, and science. This work reflects his intellectual curiosity and willingness to explore abstract and philosophical ideas.

In summary, Abdul Quayyum Khan Kundi is a multifaceted thinker and writer who has made contributions to the discussion of politics, religion, and global affairs, particularly within the context of Pakistan and the Muslim world.

You can connect with me on:

- http://abdulqkundi.com
- https://twitter.com/aqkkundi
- http://facebook.com/abdul.quayyum.khan.kundi
- https://youtube.com/@AbdulQuayyumKhanKundi

Subscribe to my newsletter:

- https://books2read.com/author/abdul-quayyum-khan-kundi/subscribe/59408

Also by Abdul Quayyum Khan Kundi

Thoughts: God, Science, & Human Nature

Religion, philosophy, and science sometimes appear to contradict each other. The deeper reality is that these operate in tandem to provide a holistic appreciation of life. Emotional crisis and physical trauma invoke questions about the purpose of life, humanity, and our place in the universe. We need to reconnect with our soul and be comfortable with the nature of things. This book is an effort to help make sense of life and our place in it.

Islamic Social Contract

"Islamic Social Contract" ventures beyond being merely a religious doctrine, aiming to present a comprehensive way of life. Rooted in the Quran and the teachings of Prophet Mohammad (PBUH), this book endeavors to construct a political framework derived from these foundational sources. It represents a proposal for the Muslim majority to contemplate and potentially embrace an alternative to the prevalent Western secular democracy.

In offering an Islamic constitution, the book tackles certain deficiencies within the Western model. It strives to address these gaps by integrating principles from Islamic teachings, thereby presenting an alternative political structure that draws from the inherent strengths and values of the Islamic tradition.

Aghosh

Collection of Urdu poetry.

Legacy of the Third Way: A Novel

A coming of age, biographical and historical fiction.
Releasing spring 2024.